W9-ASC-932

CULTURES OF THE WORLD
Honduras

Cavendish
Square
New York

243 5th Avenue, Suite 136, New York, NY 10016

Library of Congress Cataloging-in-Publication Data

Names: Wehner, Lauren. | McGaffey, Leta. | Spilling, Michael.
Title: Honduras / Lauren Wehner, Leta McGaffey and Michael Spilling.
Description: First edition. | New York : Cavendish Square, [2019] |
Includes bibliographical references and index. | Audience: Grades 6 and up.
Identifiers: LCCN 2018030832 (print) | LCCN 2018031064 (ebook) |
ISBN 9781502641038 (ebook) | ISBN 9781502641021 (library bound)
Subjects: LCSH: Honduras—Juvenile literature.
Classification: LCC F1503.2 (ebook) | LCC F1503.2 .W44 2019 (print) |
DDC 972.83--dc23
LC record available at https://lccn.loc.gov/2018030832

Editorial Director: David McNamara
Editor: Elizabeth Schmermund
Copy Editor: Nathan Heidelberger
Associate Art Director: Alan Sliwinski
Designer: Jessica Nevins
Production Coordinator: Karol Szymczuk
Photo Research: J8 Media

CONTENTS

HONDURAS TODAY

THE REPUBLIC OF HONDURAS IS A CENTRAL AMERICAN COUNTRY with a rich history, vibrant traditions, and a uniquely diverse geography. Between the deep Spanish and indigenous roots, and the winding roots of the mangrove forests, there is a growing Honduran identity. A concrete culture has been difficult to cultivate in Honduras due to the mountainous terrain and an unstable political climate, but through it all, the Honduran people have endured, and they value their traditions and their family above all else.

Honduras is split into five different regions. Unique geographical features, like mountains, beaches, dense rain forests, or fertile valleys, characterize each one. Due to the varied environments, Honduras is extremely biologically diverse, meaning that there are many different and unique plant and animal species living around the country. The varied geography and tropical climate are not only essential to the living creatures and culture of Honduras, but they are also essential to the economy. The islands, beaches, and rain forests attract tourists, while the bananas and coffee beans that grow there are exported to places like the United States.

Historically, the features of the land, as well as the ancient Mayan civilization, piqued the interest of the Spanish explorers, who were known as conquistadors. The goals of the Spanish were to explore, gather riches, conquer the people, and establish the land for Spain. Hernán Cortés was a major player in the conquest of Central America, including Honduras. With the Spanish conquest, Christianity and the Spanish language became major aspects of the developing Honduran identity. These facets of Honduran culture are still incredibly important today. The Spanish were not the only shapers of the Honduran identity, however, as the English also made their mark. Because Honduras has a major coastline in the northern region of the country, it was susceptible to English pirates and their subsequent settlement.

As the Spanish and English settled in Honduras, they brought African and Caribbean slaves with them. The African slaves, later known as Black Caribs, as well as the indigenous peoples, brought another element of tribal tradition and unique knowledge of the land to the Honduran story. The European, African, and indigenous cultures eventually blended, to the point that today you can see elements of different religions mixed together in ceremonies and festivals.

These factors, mixed with the isolation that comes from an extremely mountainous terrain, result in a fractured cultural identity. As advancements in transportation and communication have developed, and migration into the urban centers has become more prevalent, the Honduran culture has become more solidified. Television, cellular service, and internet access have become widespread, further connecting geographically distant people to each other. The rail systems and roadways have also improved, so that people are more mobile than ever. All of these factors have contributed to migration into the urban centers from the remote villages and rural areas tucked into the mountains.

Unfortunately, the migration into the cities has also been spurred by the high poverty rate in Honduras. Honduras is one of the poorest countries in Central America, and this poverty affects the vast majority of the population. While farming and agriculture are still culturally and economically significant, it has become more difficult to make a living farming. There have been efforts to increase the manufacturing and exporting power of Honduras, which has drawn many people into the cities. This is a major departure from the economic practices of the twentieth century, when the main exports were bananas and other commodity crops like coffee beans, pineapples, and mangoes. The cities are centers for education, health, and art, but they are also centers of violence, making cities like San Pedro Sula some of the most dangerous places to go in all of Central America.

There have been efforts to curb the violence in the cities, but the government of Honduras has a reputation for being embroiled in corruption. The government and central ruling powers of Honduras have been unstable since Honduras became an independent country in 1838. There has been some improvement in recent years in relation to the crime rates and the economy, but after a military coup and shady election, many Hondurans view the government as corrupt and deceitful. An upside to political unrest is that many Hondurans have come together to protest their government and fight for their rights.

A young Honduran woman processes fish for export.

Through the political unrest and poverty, the Honduran people remain resilient. They celebrate festivals, carry on traditions, and hold their families very dear. The family and familial relationships are the backbone of Honduran culture. Holidays and festivals are celebrated with loved ones. There are feasts, there is dancing, and there is merriment—all of which is done with family.

Honduras is a country with a long and complicated story, from the ancient civilizations to the present. Different groups of people have lived, fought, and settled around the region to eventually come together under one national Honduran identity. Every aspect of life in Honduras forms this identity. The land and the geography itself are as much a part of Honduran culture as its history. Its history directly influences the language and religion of the people living in Honduras today, as does the melding of traditions of the Spanish, English, African slaves, and the indigenous peoples.

GEOGRAPHY

The manteled howler monkey thrives in
the rain forests of Honduras.

1

HONDURAS IS A TROPICAL COUNTRY located in the heart of Central America. It is a bicoastal country with beautiful beaches, vast mountain ranges, and sprawling forests. The geographic regions create varying climates and living conditions for the Honduran people. Due to the mountainous terrain, many of the Honduran people live in the western half of the country, and many of the towns and cities are built into the hills or valleys of the land. San Pedro Sula, one of Honduras's largest cities, is situated in the Sula Valley due to its fertile soil and access to rivers.

With the varying environments and climates, a wide variety of biomes and habitats exist for the plants and creatures living in Honduras. Miles of coral reefs, cloud forests, deserts, and mountains are home to kinkajous, tapirs, macaws, and crocodiles alike. Tropical fruits and coffee beans are abundant in this climate and account for the majority of Honduran exports.

Although the Caribbean lowlands make up only 15 percent of the land, they support 25 percent of the population of Honduras.

THE LAND

The Republic of Honduras is a naturally diverse, mountainous country approximately the size of the state of Tennessee, with an area of 43,278 square miles (112,090 square kilometers). It is the second-largest country in Central America, bordering Guatemala in the west, El Salvador in the southwest, Nicaragua in the southeast, and the Caribbean Sea in the north, with an extensive coastline of 416 miles (669 kilometers).

There is also a small gulf in the southwest off the Pacific Ocean—the Gulf of Fonseca—with a coastline of 101 miles (163 km). Honduras stretches between 13 and 16 degrees north of the equator and between 83 and 89 degrees west longitude. Honduras is a country that boasts a diverse geography with rugged mountains, vast pine forests, idyllic beaches, flat savannas (treeless grasslands), coral reefs, and acres of fertile banana fields.

Honduras is situated just north of Nicaragua in Central America.

HIGHLANDS, LOWLANDS, COASTS, AND ISLANDS

There are four distinct geographical regions on mainland Honduras: the interior highlands, the Pacific lowlands, the Caribbean lowlands, and the Mosquito Coast. There is a fifth, separate region as well called the Bay Islands, off the north coast. Over two-thirds of Honduras consists of interior highlands featuring steep mountains and plunging valleys. Meanwhile, the Mosquito Coast, near the Nicaraguan border, is covered with dense rain forest. Along the Caribbean coast to the north, there is a stretch of long, narrow lowlands where thousands of acres of banana plantations thrive. Similarly, there is the small area of Pacific lowlands just off the Gulf of Fonseca to the south.

THE HIGHLANDS The most prominent feature of Honduran topography is the interior highlands. It is mountainous land, made up of extinct volcanoes, that stretches over 60 percent of the land. This rugged terrain is where most of the population lives, even though the mountains are difficult to travel through and to cultivate.

A major mountain range called the Cordillera Merendón runs from the southwest to the northeast, spanning the border of Honduras and Guatemala. The highest peaks are found here, including the tallest mountain, Cerro Las Minas (also called Pico Celaque), which is 9,416 feet (2,870 meters) above sea level. The less rugged Cordillera Nombre de Dios range lies south of the Caribbean shore, but still warrants attention with peaks rising to 7,988 feet (2,435 m) above sea level. Another mountain range, the Cordillera Entre Ríos, forms part of the border with Nicaragua.

Cerro Las Minas, or Pico Celaque, is the highest peak in Honduras.

Scattered throughout the interior highlands are numerous flat-floored valleys, which lie between 2,000 to 4,000 feet (610 to 1,220 m) above sea level. These fertile valleys support farming and livestock rearing due to the ashy make-up of the soil from volcanic activity. Subsistence farming has been relegated to the slopes of the valleys, while the large farming businesses work the more arable, broad valley floors in an effort to increase the country's exports.

Villages and towns, including the capital city of Tegucigalpa, have been built in the larger valleys. The Sula Valley is an extensive depression that runs from the Caribbean to the Pacific, providing a relatively convenient transportation route that also contains San Pedro Sula, the largest industrial center and second-largest city in Honduras.

PACIFIC LOWLANDS The smallest geographical region of Honduras, the Pacific lowlands, is a strip of land only 16 miles (25 km) wide on the north shore of the Gulf of Fonseca. This fertile plain was formed from volcanic soil washing down from the mountains. Cattle ranchers make use of the savannas for their grazing cattle, while mangroves grow along the shore and provide breeding grounds for shrimp and shellfish. Two islands in the Gulf of Fonseca—El Tigre and Zacate Grande—have volcanic cones that rise to over 2,296 feet (700 m) above sea level and cover the majority of both tiny islands.

Parque Nacional Montaña de Celaque contains one of the largest and purest forests in all of Central America. It is located in western Honduras, near the border with El Salvador, and is home to the country's highest peak, Cerro Las Minas. Celaque National Park is a vast cloud forest, meaning that it is a wet mountain forest that is constantly covered in low-hanging clouds. It also contains thermal springs. These clouds and springs create an extremely moist environment, which lends itself to a unique and biologically diverse ecosystem characterized by a lush canopy, mosses, orchids, and almost fifty species of mammals, like jaguars, monkeys, and pumas. The striking quetzal bird can also be seen in Celaque National Park. To see the clouds and beautiful vegetation inside the park, hikers should take a vehicle up to the visitor center to save their legs for the four- to five-hour hike that would take them into the thick of the park. Aside from the nature and creatures within the park, there is also an organic coffee farm that is open to visitors.

THE NORTH COAST Hondurans refer to the Caribbean lowlands as "the north coast," or simply "the coast." About one-quarter of the population lives in this region. It is an economically significant region for Honduras due to the alluvial plains and coastal sierras that produce rich crops of fruits and vegetables. The central part of the lowlands is narrow, only a few miles wide. To the east and west of this area, however, is a wide coastal plain where banana plantations abound. Most of the Honduran railroad system is in this region because four out of five of the major ports are located here.

MOSQUITO COAST This area of Honduras is one of Central America's last frontiers of untamed wilderness. Indigenous peoples, including the Garifuna, Pech, and Miskito, still inhabit this hot, humid region on the eastern Caribbean coast. The coast blends into mountain slopes, making it difficult to reach by road. As a result, the most common forms of transportation are airplane and boat. The dense rain forests of this region, however, have been exploited to the danger point by logging. The Caratasca Lagoon—a large body of salt water connected to the Caribbean by a narrow inlet—is located here. The Mosquito Coast was named after the Miskito Amerindians and is split between Honduras and Nicaragua. The border was hotly contested until 1850 and then resettled in 1960.

THE BAY ISLANDS Together, these islands are the jewel of the Caribbean. They are lush emerald islands crowded with palm trees and surrounded by the turquoise Caribbean Sea full of coral reefs. There are three large islands—Roatán, Utila, and Guanaja—and three smaller islands—Santa Elena (also called Helene), Morat, and Barbareta—as well as a biological reserve called the Cayos Cochinos (Hog Islands). There are also more than sixty islets scattered in the area.

The Bay Islands are the tips of ancient underwater volcanoes. These islands have a diverse geography, ranging from mountains covered in dense jungle to barrier reefs that attract divers and snorkelers from all over the world. The

The tropical island of Roatán is a popular tourist destination in Honduras.

A river flows near a small village on the outskirts of San Pedro Sula.

rainy season on the islands lasts from October to as late as February. March and August are the hottest months, but during the rest of the year, gentle sea breezes cool the air. Some of the islands are uninhabited, some have a few people living on them, and some are being developed for tourism.

Roatán is the largest, most populated, and most developed of the Bay Islands. It has a long, irregular mountain range inland, with peaks that reach 770 feet (235 m). There are also hillside pastures, limestone caves, and clumps of lush green forest. White sandy beaches and cliffs make up the north shore, while sandy inlets and bays punctuate the south shore. A beautiful, protected barrier reef that circles the island draws many tourists and scuba divers alike. The people live along the coast, many in white clapboard, tin-roofed houses on stilts. There are a few culturally rich villages. These are located near historical sites that tell interesting tales of the first pirates to invade the Bay Islands. The economic hub of Roatán is French Harbor, a town that is home to the largest fishing fleet in this area of the Caribbean, as well as schools, businesses, and the island's newest medical center.

A VAST NETWORK OF RIVERS

Rivers mark half of Honduras's borders with El Salvador and Nicaragua. Numerous rivers drain the highlands during heavy rainfall and have carved out wide, fertile valleys, but there is only one natural lake—Lake Yojoa, located in the western-central region of Honduras. The most important river is Río Ulúa, which is about 150 miles (240 km) in length and flows northeast through the Sula Valley into the Caribbean.

Due to the habitation around Honduras's rivers and the heavy rainfall, there is major risk of flooding. In some areas, such as the Biosfera del Río Plátano, river travel is the main way to penetrate the region.

In October 1998, a terrible natural disaster hit Honduras as Hurricane Mitch rampaged across the country. The rare class 5 hurricane, with winds of up to 180 miles per hour (290 kilometers per hour), began its destruction of Honduras when it sat for two days over Guanaja, one of the Bay Islands, which was devastated. By the time it reached the mainland, it was classified as a tropical storm. However, the amount of rain that was dumped onto almost every inch of Honduras (up to 4 feet [1.2 m] in many areas) created mudslides that literally buried whole villages, highways, and roads, and wiped out most bridges in the country. The cap of an extinct volcano fell off due to the rains and wiped out the villages in its path. Honduran cities and villages were left totally isolated except by air.

The storm killed an estimated 6,600 people in Honduras. A week after the storm had subsided, 11,998 people were still missing and 1.4 million were left homeless and living in crowded shelters on high land. The hurricane wreaked havoc on the fertile Aguan and Sula Valleys, destroying thousands of acres of banana and palm plantations. Approximately 70 percent of the nation's crops were destroyed—some fruit companies on the Caribbean coast lost 100 percent of their crops. Over 60 percent of the nation's infrastructure, including major bridges, was demolished. The total damage to infrastructure alone, not including loss in exports, was estimated at $2 billion.

In the wake of Hurricane Mitch, Honduras is now the most advanced country in Central America in regard to emergency management and preparedness, through the Permanent Contingency Commission of Honduras. This is an essential organization due to the country's active volcanoes, and the constant threat of hurricanes, tsunamis, and flooding.

CLIMATE

The interior highlands have tropical wet and dry seasons. Almost all the rain falls during the wet season from May to September. In the northern and eastern coastal and alluvial plains, the average annual rainfall ranges from 70 to 110 inches (178 to 280 centimeters) or more. Tegucigalpa, located in the highlands, has a pleasant climate ranging from 86 degrees Fahrenheit (30 degrees Celsius) in April, the warmest month, to 73°F (23°C) in January, the coolest month. As elevation increases, temperature decreases. Above 6,562 feet (2,000 m), there can be frost after a cold night.

The Pacific lowlands also have wet and dry seasons, with year-round high temperatures between 82°F (28°C) and 90°F (32°C). The dry season occurs between November and April, usually the hottest months of the year. During the rainy season, the high humidity makes the heat uncomfortable.

The Caribbean lowlands have a tropical wet climate with high temperatures and humidity and rainfall year-round. These conditions have made the Caribbean lowlands ideal for growing bananas and pineapples, which need warm, wet weather. The only relief from the hot weather comes in December or January, when there are high winds but only slightly cooler temperatures.

The Caribbean coast is particularly prone to hurricanes and tropical storms because Honduras lies within the hurricane belt (an area of the Atlantic Ocean prone to hurricanes). These storms usually travel inland from the Caribbean. Hurricanes occasionally form over the Pacific, but these are generally less severe and rarely make landfall.

TROPICAL FLORA

Honduras has a wide variety of vegetation due to its tropical climate and varying environmental regions ranging from beaches to forests to deserts. Honduras's forests have only been set aside as national parks and biological reserves since the 1980s in an effort to protect the trees from loggers and industrialization. On top of mountains and along ridges are cloud forests. These "weeping woods," as they are called, catch the moisture in the air, creating an ideal environment for ferns, vines, orchids, and broadleaf plants to grow. A rich layer of decaying matter covers the forest floor, and bromeliads (a type of flowering plant) flourish in the crooks of trees. Many varieties of wild avocado grow in abundance in varying moisture conditions.

Near these humid peaks are patches of desert that were created as a result of the cloud forests capturing all of the moisture. At lower elevations, pines and firs cover the mountainsides. In the savannas of the northeast are acacias and cacti, while in the warmer and wetter lowlands there are mahogany, Spanish cedar, rosewood, palm trees, and mangroves. Besides avocados, tropical fruit that grow and thrive include tamarinds, mangoes, pineapples, guavas, papayas, and of course, bananas.

EXOTIC FAUNA

Honduras's great variety in climate allows for a wide variety of mammals, fish, birds, amphibians, reptiles, and insects to live in the region. Honduras has many of the forest animals that are found in the United States, but it also has some exotic mammals. Among the familiar creatures are raccoons, coyotes,

A spotted jaguar lounges in the shade of the Honduran rain forest.

While quetzals and rainbow macaws are some of the most visually stunning creatures native to Honduras, true beauty and power can be seen in the wild jaguar. This predatory feline can be distinguished by its stocky frame and spotted fur. The jaguar is one of the top predators in its habitat.

Kinkajous are native to Honduras and are listed as a protected species.

armadillos, foxes, squirrels, and porcupines. Some of the more exotic mammals include brocket deer, monkeys, jaguars, and other large cats. There are also animals found only in tropical America, such as the kinkajou, a tree-dwelling mammal with brown fur and a prehensile tail, also called the honey bear.

Honduras is home to a wide variety of reptiles and amphibians as well. Snakes, including the boa, worm, coral, bushmaster, rattlesnake, and fer-de-lance, are abundant, and there are also many species of brightly colored frogs and toads. Crocodiles, caimans, and salamanders live in and near the water. Many turtles, such as the huge leatherback, live either in the sea or on the shore. Lizards are found everywhere. Little hand-sized geckos make their home anywhere, and iguanas can grow up to 6 feet (1.8 m) long.

Lake Yojoa has large black bass that provide excellent game fishing. Sharks, catfish, barracudas, grouper, and mackerel are just a few examples of the ocean life found in the Caribbean Sea and the Gulf of Fonseca. There are mollusks such as snails, as well as crustaceans such as lobsters and freshwater crabs.

More than seven hundred species of birds are found in Honduras. Of note are swallows, the green ibis, the tiger heron, spotted wood-quails, cuckoos, macaws, quetzals, and a beautiful cloud forest trogon with iridescent red and green feathers and long tail feathers that arc like a peacock's. The scarlet macaw is the national bird of Honduras.

There are many species of butterflies, moths, beetles, spiders, bees, wasps, ants, flies, and mosquitoes, many of them brightly colored.

NOTABLE CITIES AND TOWNS

Honduras is the only Central American country that has most of its urban population distributed between two large city centers: Tegucigalpa and San Pedro Sula. Although Honduras is still primarily an agrarian society, these two cities have grown considerably since the 1920s as Hondurans have

migrated from rural areas to urban areas to find jobs. The two cities contrast dramatically: Tegucigalpa is the political capital, whereas San Pedro Sula is the industrial and commercial center. Other cities in Honduras include La Ceiba, Santa Rosa de Copán, El Progreso, and Puerto Cortés, home of the country's busiest port.

The majority of cities and towns are located in the western region of Honduras. Many of them are set amid splendid countryside and have interesting historical and native legends. Small towns such as La Esperanza, Gracias, and Santa Lucía attract a steady stream of tourists.

TEGUCIGALPA The capital city of Honduras, Tegucigalpa, is built into the hills of the central highlands. It became the permanent capital city in 1880.

Tegucigalpa has the flavor of a small colonial city, with brightly colored houses built into the hillsides and narrow, winding streets. At the center of

Hondurans stroll in the bustling city of Tegucigalpa.

For all practical purposes Tegucigalpa is the capital of Honduras. However, the Honduran constitution states, "The cities of Tegucigalpa and Comayagüela, jointly, constitute the Capital of the Republic." This joint capital is also known as distrito central *(central district). The presidential and legislative palaces are located in Tegucigalpa. It is one of the only capital cities in the world without a railroad.*

the city are Spanish colonial churches; many government buildings, including the National Palace and the Presidential Palace; and numerous schools. This landmark historic center includes the Plaza Morazán, often called Parque Central, with a statue of the national hero Francisco Morazán.

Overlooking Tegucigalpa is the United Nations National Park on Picacho Mountain. This park is recognized for its magnificent gardens of tropical plants and flowers, including beautiful Honduran orchids. Residents of Tegucigalpa flock to the park on Sundays and use the outdoor grills for picnics.

Tegucigalpa experienced near-crippling population growth beginning in the 1950s, when the population increased by 75 percent. The population increased even further during the 1990s. As of 2018, it is estimated that more than 1.3 million people live in Tegucigalpa's sprawling metropolitan area. Many of them today still have inadequate housing and either do not have running water or receive an inadequate supply. In 1998, Hurricane Mitch worsened conditions, leaving tens of thousands of people homeless.

SAN PEDRO SULA San Pedro Sula is the bustling center of business transactions, or the industrial capital of Honduras. It is located in the flat, fertile Sula Valley surrounded by banana plantations, and it has over eight hundred thousand residents. The population of this city is more multicultural than the rest of the country. The San Pedranos, as they call themselves, are friendly, outgoing, and helpful to foreign visitors.

San Pedro Sula was founded in June 1536 as an agricultural town. Its importance increased quickly with the growth of fruit companies on the north

coast, and the city has become the center of agricultural business for the region. San Pedro Sula is perhaps the fastest-growing city in Central America.

The city has modern glass towers as well as residential areas where stately homes with green lawns offer an old-world charm and people stroll along tree-lined avenues in the evenings. However, the city of San Pedro Sula is also one of the most dangerous cities in all of Central America. In 2013, it was known as the murder capital of the world due to high murder rates and gang activity. As of 2016, murder rates have gone down and the city is beginning to regain its sense of community.

PUERTO CORTÉS The largest and most important port in Honduras is also the most modern port in Central America, with large container facilities that stretch for 16 miles (26 km) along the bay. It is only a two-day sail from New Orleans or Miami. Puerto Cortés grew quickly in order to accommodate the export of bananas, and later as a center for oil refining. Bananas, coffee, coconuts, hardwood, and flour are the principal exports from Puerto Cortés. It also has numerous manufacturing companies that export products such as baseballs and luxury sailing boats. Puerto Cortés serves as the main seaport of San Pedro Sula and the Sula Valley.

LA CEIBA Nestled on the narrow coastal plain between the Cordillera Nombre de Dios and the Caribbean coast, La Ceiba is surrounded by banana and pineapple plantations. It has an international airport and many people go there to visit as a starting point to get to the Bay Islands. La Ceiba got its name from a large ceiba, or silk-cotton, tree that used to stand on the coast before the development of the docks. Traders used to congregate there to buy and sell in the shade of the big tree. As one of the Caribbean's major ports, it exports bananas, pineapples, citrus fruits, coconuts, abaca fiber, fish, meat, coffee, and lumber. La Ceiba is an ethnic melting pot, with Garifunas, Bay Islanders, Miskito Natives, and an important expatriate community living there. La Ceiba is famous for the Cangrejal River and its outstanding white-water rafting and kayaking. Hot springs are abundant along the north coast of Honduras, and

La Ceiba is no exception, with lovely natural hot-water springs within nearby Nombre de Dios National Park.

COLONIAL TOWNS Many towns in Honduras were established during the Spanish colonial period. A few grew to the extent that they are now for government, industrial, or commercial reasons. Other towns are better known as colonial heritage sites.

Comayagua, about 52 road miles (84 km) northwest of Tegucigalpa, was once the capital of Honduras. It is famous for having numerous churches, including the Iglesia la Merced, the first church built in the country during the sixteenth century. The city is not to be confused with Comayagüela, which today is the joint capital of the country, along with Tegucigalpa.

Considered the center of western Honduras, Santa Rosa de Copán is surrounded by mountains and national parks. It is a small, cool, very Spanish

Iglesia El Calvario stands in the capital city of Tegucigalpa.

mountain town with El Calvario, a two-hundred-year-old church; cobblestone streets; and tile-roofed houses. It was once famous for its tobacco farms, but today it is better known for its coffee. Santa Rosa is now the chief commercial center of western Honduras. Major industries include tobacco blending and cigar making, sugar refining, and mat weaving. Lumber, furniture, leather products, clothing, and beverages are also produced.

Suyapa, just outside the capital, is called the religious capital of Honduras. A legend here tells of the miraculous discovery by a peasant of a tiny clay statue of the Virgin of Suyapa, the patron saint of Honduras.

Trujillo, located close to where Christopher Columbus first landed on mainland America, was the first capital of Honduras. Spaniards fought off pirates from a Spanish fort there. The ruins of this fort overlook the bay. Trujillo is also known for its beaches and natural hot springs.

INTERNET LINKS

http://www.honduras.com/cities
This official site offers a breakdown of cities with an article guide for each city listed.

http://traveltips.usatoday.com/native-animals-plants -honduras-63620.html
This *USA Today* article showcases native animals and plants in Honduras.

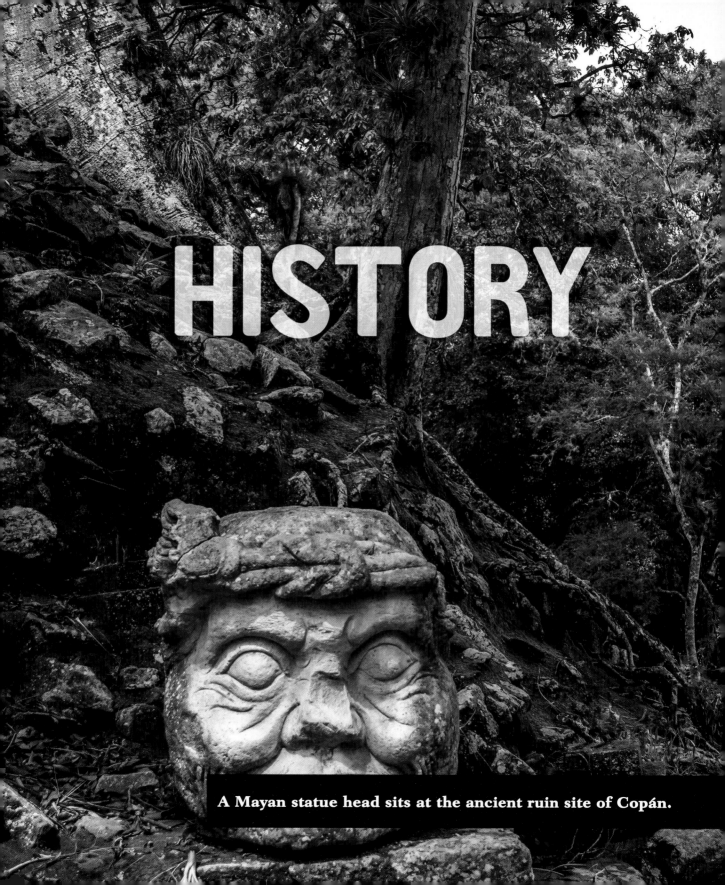

HISTORY

A Mayan statue head sits at the ancient ruin site of Copán.

2

HONDURAS HAS A LONG AND storied history full of rich cultures, conquest, and the building of a cultural identity. Starting with the Mayan people, Honduras was a major center of the classic period. The Maya and other indigenous groups made Honduras their home until the Spanish conquistadors claimed Honduras for Spain, creating a new cultural legacy. As Spanish became the official language and new settlers arrived, a new Honduran identity was forged. Recent natural disasters, political unrest, and corruption have also made a lasting impression on the Honduran people, but they continue to grow and embrace their Honduran culture and identity.

Honduras was populated by the Maya, and the city of Copán became a major Mayan city-state of the classic period (300-900 CE). The last known ruler of Copán began his reign in 822 CE.

ANCIENT SOCIETIES

Because Central America is a midway point between North and South America, people of various cultures have passed through Honduras over the centuries. Many of them eventually settled down in this region. Before Europeans reached Honduras, the land was populated by groups of people who spoke unrelated languages and whose customs were different.

Over ten thousand years ago, people first arrived from possibly Asia or Polynesia. These settlers were probably hunters who lived in caves or simple dwellings and who followed their prey. Thousands of years later, agriculture was introduced. The first crop was most likely maize (corn), which is still a staple today. Along with maize, beans, squash, chili peppers, and cotton were probably the most important crops for cultivation.

The most advanced and notable early inhabitants were related to the Maya of the Yucatán and Guatemala. The Mayan civilization reached Honduras in the fifth century CE and spread rapidly through the Río Motagua Valley in western Honduras. The Maya established extensive networks of trade throughout the region, spanning as far as central Mexico. The money of the Maya was probably the cacao bean, which is still a local product. The ancient western Honduran city of Copán became a center for Mayan astronomical studies, mathematics, and art. One of the longest hieroglyphic inscriptions was found at Copán.

Copán was apparently abandoned at the height of Mayan civilization, as were many of the major Mayan centers. There are extensive ruins there today. Many Maya stayed in the region, but the high priests and rulers suddenly vanished. From this point on, Honduras was dominated by one indigenous group after another. These groups were often hostile toward each other. Because the different indigenous groups were always in conflict, there was no distinct center of authority in the region at the time of conquest by the Spanish. By subduing and allying themselves with different indigenous groups, the Spanish were able to take over the region.

COLUMBUS AND THE CONQUISTADORS

First contact with the Spanish occurred in 1502, during Christopher Columbus's fourth and final expedition to the Americas. Columbus sailed past the Bay Islands, and it is believed he made contact with indigenous nobility there. He then sailed on to the mainland coast of Central America and set foot in Punta

Caxinas on August 14, 1502. He named the place "Honduras," a loose translation of "deep waters," which was a reference to the depth of the bay off the north coast. There was little European exploration of Honduras for the next two decades.

Interest in Honduras only began as a result of rivalries among Spanish military leaders in Central America, who were too far away for the emperor in Spain to govern. The men sent to explore, conquer, and claim Central America for the Spanish Empire were known as conquistadors. An expedition headed north from Panama, and in 1522, Gil González Dávila discovered and named the Gulf of Fonseca in honor of the Spanish bishop Juan Rodríguez de Fonseca. Expeditions organized by Hernán Cortés (1485—1547) also came down from Mexico. One of these expeditions, led by Cristóbal de Olid, first conquered Honduran territory and established a settlement there on May 3, 1524.

Christopher Columbus (1451-1506) was an Italian explorer who sailed and explored for Spain.

Rival Spanish expeditions invaded Honduras and fought to become supreme, not only over the indigenous people, but among themselves. Hernán Cortés left Mexico in 1524 to deal with the conflict in Honduras and establish his authority. He temporarily restored some order by getting a few indigenous chiefs to submit to his authority, and then he began to set up Spanish towns. As soon as he left nearly two years later, the strife resumed.

SPANISH COLONIZATION

By the early 1530s, the indigenous people of Honduras were being killed off by disease, mistreatment, and shipment to the Caribbean Islands as slaves. The discovery of gold and silver in Honduras in 1536 attracted new settlers who demanded local labor for their mines. This forced labor led to a major uprising by the indigenous people led by Lempira, a young chieftain of the Lenca tribe. His courage inspired many other native groups to revolt, and the battle raged for two years. Lempira was eventually murdered by the Spanish.

Indigenous resistance died down after Lempira's revolt failed. The revolt had resulted in the deaths of even more of the native population. In 1539, an

Lempira (d. 1537) was the chief and an esteemed warrior of the Lenca tribe. He is considered a great hero in Honduras for organizing and executing a revolt against the Spanish in the 1530s. His name lives on as the word for the main unit of currency in modern-day Honduras.

The revolt was essentially a failure, but Lempira unified more than two hundred Native tribes that had been ancient rivals in order to offer an organized resistance against penetration by the Spanish conquistadors. Lempira acted as a general to his troops. In the village of Etempica, he announced his plans to expel the Spaniards and gave instructions to all his allies for a general uprising. Together, they created an impenetrable fortress with trenches and fortifications on top of the great rock of Cerquín. Lempira's troops were to attack on his signal, which came in the form of killing three unsuspecting Spaniards in the area.

The Spanish gathered their forces and stormed Cerquín, but the fortress held. Lempira ordered further attacks. Comayagua was set on fire, causing the Spanish inhabitants to flee to Gracias, where they were threatened further by the surrounding tribes. Captain Alonso de Cáceres of Spain soon called for a peace conference with Lempira. During the meeting, Lempira allegedly reaffirmed his desire to fight, and in doing so was shot in the head by a hidden marksman. With the death of their leader, the unified warriors fled or surrendered to the Spanish.

estimated fifteen thousand indigenous people were under Spanish control, but two years later, after the revolt, there were only approximately eight thousand still alive.

The Spanish settlement of Honduras expanded in the 1540s as the fighting among rival Spaniards decreased, and the first bishop of Honduras was named. Comayagua was made the capital of Honduras on December 20, 1557, replacing Trujillo. The key economic activity was mining for gold and silver, but some

cattle ranching began as well. The indigenous people who were brought to work in the mines came from different villages all over the region. Because the indigenous population was now so small, the Spanish needed a larger labor force. Thus, African slaves were brought in. Everyone was forced to communicate in the language of the masters—Spanish. The old ways were mixed with the new Spanish ways, and a new culture was born.

However, gold and silver finds became scarce, and mining began to decline in the 1560s. Honduras became a province of the Captaincy General of Guatemala and remained so until it won independence from Spain in 1821. The discovery of silver in the 1570s briefly revived the economy, and Tegucigalpa began to rival Comayagua in size and importance. Mining efforts were hampered by the

This illustration shows African slaves in the Caribbean processing sugarcane. Sugar was a commodity good in Europe and was, therefore, in high demand.

José Trinidad Cabañas (1805–1871) is considered a hero for his attempts to reunite the Central American federal government. He was president of Honduras for two separate terms—March 1 to July 6, 1852, and December 31, 1853, to June 6, 1855. Cabañas was creole (mixed race), the son of José María Cabañas and Juana María Fiallos. He was a liberal politician whose role in Honduran history began during the civil war of 1826–1829, when he was second-in-command to Francisco Morazán.

His second term as president was noteworthy for the very first attempt to build a railroad in Central America. He was supported by the Honduran people, but his liberal beliefs and their support were not acceptable to the conservatives who then held power in Guatemala. Interference in Guatemalan affairs led to his overthrow by the Guatemalans in 1855.

Cabañas fled to El Salvador, where he remained politically active. He was responsible for a political uprising in El Salvador as late as 1865.

José Cecilio del Valle is considered a hero in Honduras, even though he lived in Guatemala. He wrote the declaration of Central America's independence from Spain in 1821.

limited size of gold and silver deposits, a lack of capital and labor, the rugged terrain, and bureaucratic regulations and incompetence. By the seventeenth century, Honduras was being neglected and became a poor Spanish colony. A major problem for the Spanish emerged in the seventeenth century in the form of English pirates along the Caribbean coast. Eventually, the English began to settle on the Bay Islands and along the coast. Spain later regained control of the Caribbean coast, but the English settlers remained, further blending the culture.

INDEPENDENCE AND INSTABILITY

Spain granted Honduras independence, along with the other Central American provinces, on September 15, 1821. Honduras and the other Central American countries briefly became a part of the Mexican empire, but they broke away from Mexican rule after a coup in 1823 and established the United Provinces of Central America, with the capital in Guatemala City.

The first president, Manuel José Arce (1786—1847), was elected in 1825. Francisco Morazán, a Honduran military hero, was elected president of the federation in 1830. In 1834, he moved the capital to San Salvador, located in present-day El Salvador.

The 1830s saw constant conflict between the Liberal and Conservative Parties of the region. After a Conservative revolt led by Rafael Carrera (1814—1865) in 1838, the federation was dissolved. Honduras declared independence on November 15, 1838. By January 1839, it had adopted a constitution, although there was little sense of nationhood. All attempts to restore the federation after this 1838 split failed.

For Honduras, the period of federation had been a time of local rivalries, ideological disputes, political chaos, and the disruption of its already fragile economy. This instability attracted ambitious politicians from within and outside Central America. For most of the rest of the nineteenth century, El Salvador, Guatemala, and Nicaragua interfered in Honduras's internal affairs. Six constitutions were implemented, and presidents were imposed and deposed by Nicaragua and Guatemala. The frequent changes of government made Honduras unstable.

Bananas, a staple crop and major export for Honduras, are being harvested in this photo.

THE BANANA REPUBLIC

In the end of the 1890s, banana traders Joseph, Luca, and Felix Vaccaro, together with Salvador D'Antoni, in New Orleans, Louisiana, looked to Honduras as a reliable supplier of commercially grown bananas. The brothers founded the Standard Fruit Company, which is known today as the Dole Food Company. In the north, along the Caribbean coast, banana plantations began operation. Honduras soon became the world's leading exporter of bananas. The banana companies became more important than the government for many Hondurans because of their domination of commercial life in the area and worker welfare system. Bananas remained the mainstay of the modern economy for many years, and the fruit companies held a high degree of influence over the government, leading to Honduras's nickname, the "Banana Republic."

THE GREAT BANANA STRIKE OF 1954

In 1954, Honduran workers at a Caribbean port asked for overtime wages for loading bananas onto a boat on a Sunday. Their request was refused, but they loaded the boat anyway. The following Sunday, a similar incident occurred. Officials noticed a slowdown in work but foolishly ignored it. As the unrest grew, President Juan Manuel Gálvez Durón became concerned and sent soldiers to the Caribbean coast. This action angered the workers, and within a week one of the banana companies had lost all its workers. The strike spread to other banana companies, a tobacco plant, a mining company, and several clothing factories, all American-owned. The strikers held out for three months. When officials finally made concessions, work resumed with shorter hours, overtime pay, medical benefits, and paid vacations. Workers in Honduras had learned that they were a powerful political force.

TWENTIETH-CENTURY HONDURAS

In Tegucigalpa, power remained unstable, and revolts repeatedly broke out against the government. Nicaragua became more and more involved in Honduras in the early twentieth century. When its army invaded the country in February 1907, the US government intervened to protect the North American banana trade. President William Howard Taft sent US Marines to Puerto Cortés in 1911 to ward off Nicaraguan forces.

In the 1923 election for a new Honduran president, no candidate won a majority of the votes, leaving the country on the brink of civil war. The United

Border disputes have long been a problem in Central America. Honduras has rarely been the aggressor, but in 1969 a border dispute with El Salvador erupted into a brief war. The Honduran government believed that Salvadorans had taken advantage of the open border with Honduras and had gained property under the agrarian reforms that were taking place in Honduras. This land

was only supposed to go to people who were Honduran by birth.

The dispute is called the Football (Soccer) War because, at the time, Honduras and El Salvador were engaged in a three-game elimination match for the 1970 World Cup preliminaries. Fights broke out at the games, and both countries were insulted and enraged. Honduras decided to suspend trade with El Salvador. Salvadoran troops invaded Honduras, but the fighting was ended after two weeks due to intervention by the Organization of American States. The territorial dispute was finally resolved by the International Court of Justice (ICJ) in 1992, which awarded most of the disputed territory to Honduras. In 1998, the two countries signed a treaty to confirm the borders determined by the ICJ, and in 2006 the demarcation was completed.

States stepped in again, and a new election was held in which the newly formed conservative National Party took power. In 1932, General Tiburcio Carías Andino (1876—1969) was chosen as president in a peaceful, fair election. He remained in power until 1949, ruling with an authoritarian hand. Early in the Carías regime, Panama disease dramatically damaged the banana industry, while the Great Depression and World War II cut off the banana trade and the fruit rotted on the docks.

In 1954, banana workers went on strike following a labor dispute, causing a severe strain on the nation's economy. Initial government efforts to end the strike failed, and work stoppages spread to other industries. The strike

General Tiburcio Carías Andino (1876-1969) was the president of Honduras from 1933 to 1949.

ended when workers were granted better benefits and the right to bargain. After decades of domination, the strike decreased the power of the fruit companies.

In 1957, yet another constitution was enacted, and Ramón Villeda Morales (1909—1971) of the Liberal Party became president. Under Villeda, many schools were built and labor rights were strengthened. A social security system was installed, but it provided medical care and pensions for only a limited number of workers. In December 1960, the Central American Common Market was formed to aid trade between the countries of the region, and restrictions on imports were lifted. Many products that used to be imported were now regionally made, increasing domestic manufacturing. However, after years where the only development was around the coastal areas by the fruit companies, Honduras lacked a wider road network, a railroad system, and a proper banking system. Most of the factories in Central America were established in Guatemala, El Salvador, and Costa Rica—Honduras was left behind.

On October 3, 1963, a military coup put air force colonel Oswaldo López Arellano in power. Congress was dissolved, the constitution was suspended, and planned elections were canceled. The United States promptly broke off diplomatic relations with Honduras. In 1978, a new junta (military committee) headed by General Policarpo Paz García seized the government, promising to return Honduras to civilian rule. In April 1980, military rule began to wind down; a constituent assembly was convened and an election was planned.

Meanwhile violent revolutions were occurring in neighboring Nicaragua and El Salvador. The United States supplied weapons to Honduras in response to the left-wing Sandinista victory in Nicaragua, and the US military staged maneuvers in Honduras to scare off any potential Nicaraguan incursions. After the conflict, the decrease in US military spending in Honduras left the country in an economic crisis once again. Rafael Leonardo Callejas Romero (b. 1943) of the National Party scored a clear victory in the 1989 election, and he began

LEADERS OF HONDURAS SINCE 1933

Tiburcio Carías Andino *1933–1949*
Juan Manuel Gálvez Durón *1949–1954*
Julio Lozano Díaz *1954–1956*
Roque Jacinto Rodríguez Herrera *1956–1957*
Ramón Villeda Morales *1957–1963*
Oswaldo López Arellano *1963–1965, 1965–1971*
Ramón Ernesto Cruz Uclés *1971–1972*
Oswaldo López Arellano *1972–1975*
Juan Alberto Melgar Castro *1975–1978*
Policarpo Paz García *1978–1980, 1980–1982*
Roberto Suazo Córdova *1982–1986*
José Azcona del Hoyo *1986–1990*
Rafael Leonardo Callejas Romero *1990–1994*
Carlos Roberto Reina Idiáquez *1994–1998*
Carlos Roberto Flores Facussé *1998–2002*
Ricardo Maduro Joest *2002–2006*
Manuel Zelaya *2006–2009*
Roberto Micheletti* *2009–2010*
Porfirio Lobo Sosa *2010–2014*
Juan Orlando Hernández *2014–Present*

*interim

to deal with the economic situation. The rising cost of living contributed to his party's defeat in the 1993 election. Carlos Roberto Reina Idiáquez of the Liberal Party, who became president, continued the work begun by Callejas. He was succeeded in January 1998 by Carlos Roberto Flores Facussé, also of the Liberal Party.

Just when the political climate appeared to have settled, disaster struck in the form of Hurricane Mitch in November 1998. The storm left Honduras in dire straits, with the country's crucial farming industry severely damaged and the country's infrastructure weakened.

HONDURAS TODAY

Former president Manuel Zelaya

In recent years, crime and gang violence have become serious problems in Honduras. In 2001, Ricardo Maduro Joest was elected president. He introduced tough policies to fight increasing crime and corruption. In 2005, Manuel Zelaya was elected president on an anticrime, antigang platform.

However, on June 28, 2009, President Zelaya was forced into exile by a military-backed coup. The coup occurred because of a disagreement between the president and his political opponents over changes he wanted to make to the constitution through a referendum scheduled for June 28. The Honduran Congress, Supreme Court, and military all declared the planned poll illegal. Zelaya's opponents feared the changes to the constitution would allow the sitting president to extend his presidency, which was unlawful under the existing constitution. The head of Congress, Roberto Micheletti, assumed the role of interim president of Honduras. Protesting Hondurans took to the streets, with groups for and against the coup. Although Zelaya maintained a great deal of international support, the new government blocked attempts for him to return.

Porfirio Lobo Sosa of the National Party of Honduras was elected president in November 2009 after Zelaya was ousted. He won with 56 percent of the vote, but his legitimacy as president was still questioned by rioters, human rights activists, and leaders of neighboring countries due to the military coup that removed the previous administration and inaccurate reports of voter turnout.

The Honduran constitution has had a strict one-term president policy since the 1980s, which has made the election of the current president, Juan Orlando Hernández, especially important. Hernández was elected president in 2013 to serve the 2014 term. He ran with the National Party of Honduras after beating Ricardo Álvarez in an internal election to be the party's candidate. Álvarez demanded a recount, citing corruption, but was denied. Thanks to changes made to the constitution in 2015, through a close vote by the Supreme Court, Hernández was permitted to run for reelection, and he subsequently won in 2017. The inauguration was plagued by protests where thirty people were killed and accusations of fraud. His presidency is still hotly contested.

Juan Orlando Hernández (1968–) was inaugurated as president in 2014.

INTERNET LINKS

https://www.aljazeera.com/news/2018/01/honduras-president-hernandez-sworn-protests-180127172421884.html
This article from *Al Jazeera* is about the inauguration of President Juan Orlando Hernández in 2018.

http://www.revuemag.com/2016/09/jose-cecilio-del-valle-of-guatemala
This article from *Revue* magazine explores the life of José Cecilio del Valle.

https://specialcollections.tulane.edu/archon/?p=collections/findingaid&id=84&q=&rootcontentid=79860
This site offers an extensive history of the banana trade in Honduras and the Standard Fruit Company.

https://www.youtube.com/watch?v=FVshtHUysBc
This video features footage from the Football War with some commentary.

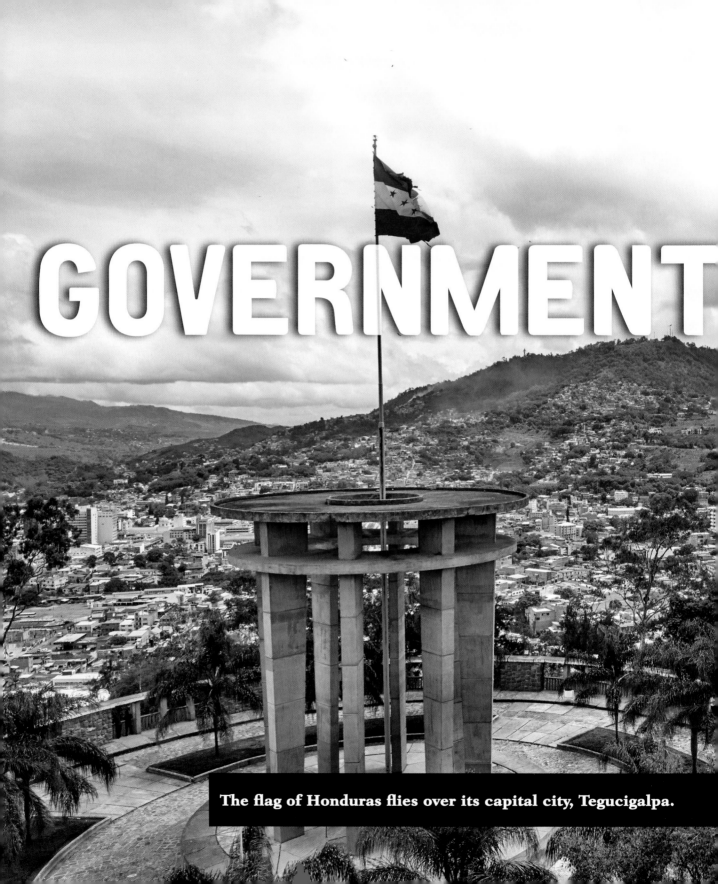

GOVERNMENT

The flag of Honduras flies over its capital city, Tegucigalpa.

3

THROUGHOUT ITS HISTORY Honduras has struggled to maintain political stability. The country has often had a chaotic array of interest groups vying for influence, with the military sometimes seizing power. However, in the early 2000s, the political process became more stable, and democratic elections generally happened peacefully and openly. This changed in 2009 with the military coup that overthrew President Manuel Zelaya. Later, the election of President Juan Orlando Hernández was steeped in accusations of corruption and fraud. These accusations continued with the second-term election of Hernández in 2017. Honduras is currently divided over the legitimacy of its leader and his alleged crimes.

President Juan Orlando Hernández is the first two-term president of Honduras since 1980, when Honduras transitioned from a dictatorship into a democracy.

NATIONAL GOVERNMENT

Honduras is a democratic republic that abides by its constitution. Honduras's national government is divided into three branches: executive, legislative, and judicial. Each branch is supposed to be autonomous, but in reality the executive branch dominates the legislative and judicial branches. There is also a group called the National Elections Tribunal that functions as an independent division with jurisdiction throughout the country.

CONSTITUTION The present constitution of Honduras, the sixteenth since independence from Spain, was adopted on January 20, 1982, one week after almost twenty years of military rule ended. The Honduran constitution is seen more as a political ideal than a legal instrument, and it has been changed in detail many times. This constitution establishes three separate branches of government and provides for an independent elections tribunal that handles national elections. It also protects basic human rights, women's right to vote, child and labor rights, freedom of speech, and freedom of the press. Issues of nationality, social security, health, education, and housing are dealt with in detail.

THE EXECUTIVE BRANCH The executive branch is headed by the president, who is assisted by at least twelve cabinet ministers. The president is elected by a simple majority every four years and, until the 2017 election, could not run for a succeeding term. Presidents have been overthrown by military coups as well.

The responsibilities of the president include organizing, directing, and promoting economic, education, health, and foreign policies. The president has the power to veto or approve laws passed by the National Congress with a few exceptions, such as constitutional amendments. The president is also given the military title of general commander.

THE LEGISLATIVE BRANCH The legislative branch consists of the unicameral National Congress—128 deputies are elected every four years at the same time as the president. The members are selected proportionally by administrative departments. The National Congress conducts legislative functions during regular annual sessions from January to October. Its roles

Honduras introduced an electoral law in May 2004 that states that at least 30 percent of candidates for the National Congress and the municipal councils must be female. No political party has managed to completely comply with this rule. As of 2018, however, they are close, with thirty-three female representatives, bringing female representation to 25.8 percent. In 2009, Patricia Rodas became the foreign minister, and in 2010, María Antonieta de Bográn became the first female vice president.

are to approve choices of the president, appoint committees to study issues that come before the legislature, elect government officials, and approve the national budget, international treaties, and taxes.

THE JUDICIAL BRANCH The judicial branch of the government consists of the Supreme Court of Justice, courts of appeal, courts of first instance, and justices of the peace. The Supreme Court is the court of last resort. Fifteen judges are elected by the National Congress for a seven-year term. It has fourteen constitutional powers and duties and is divided into four chambers—civil, criminal, labor, and constitutional—with smaller groups of justices assigned to each chamber. Courts of appeal have three-judge panels who hear appeals from all lower courts. The courts of first instance serve as trial courts for serious civil and criminal cases. Justices of the peace serve in each department of the country as investigators of minor cases.

The coat of arms of Honduras was created in 1825 to commemorate the freedom and independence of Honduras.

THE NATIONAL ELECTIONS TRIBUNAL Since Honduras returned to civilian democratic rule in 1982, national elections have been held every four years to elect the president, the National Congress, and municipal officials. The National Elections Tribunal is an independent body that is responsible for organizing and conducting elections. The National Registry of Persons works under the National Elections Tribunal and is responsible for issuing identity cards to all Hondurans (these are also voter registration cards) and conducting a census before each election.

The 2009 coup against President Zelaya severely fractured the Liberal Party, leading to the creation of the Liberty and Refoundation Party. Hondurans were also deeply affected by the economic troubles during Zelaya's administration, which caused many to change long-standing party allegiance. Previously, there were few ideological differences between the Liberal Party and the National Party in Honduras, and allegiance to one group or the other was often based on family tradition. The Liberal Party was stronger in urban areas and the more developed northern departments. The National Party, on the other hand, was stronger in more rural areas and the less developed southern agricultural departments.

LOCAL GOVERNMENT

Honduras is divided into eighteen departments (provinces), which are subdivided into 298 municipalities (*municipios*). A municipality may include more than one city. There is also a Central District made up of Tegucigalpa and Comayagüela. The president freely appoints and removes governors for each department. Departmental governors are an extension of the executive branch of the national government. Each governor may freely appoint or remove a secretary to assist him or her. A municipality is administered by a mayor (*alcalde*) and a council elected every four years at the same time as the president. The council varies in size depending on the population of the municipality.

POLITICAL PARTIES

Two parties have traditionally been dominant—the Liberal Party of Honduras (Partido Liberal de Honduras—PLH) and the National Party of Honduras (Partido Nacional de Honduras—PNH). These were the only two official parties from 1902 to 1948, which laid the groundwork for the present-day system. The PLH was established in 1891 under the leadership of Policarpo Bonilla Vásquez and had its origins in the liberal reform efforts of the late nineteenth century. The PNH was formed in 1902 when a group broke off from the PLH. In 1963, it became aligned with the military.

Since the 1980s, Honduras has had a very tense relationship with its southern neighbor, Nicaragua. In the 1980s, Nicaragua was governed by the left-wing Sandinistas, while Honduras's government and military were heavily backed by the United States, which opposed the Sandinistas. For many years, one of the problems in this relationship was a disagreement over the two countries' maritime boundary in the Caribbean Sea. Both sides claimed fishing rights in the area and resorted to seizing each other's fishing vessels in the struggle for territory. However, in 2007, the dispute was settled by the International Court of Justice (ICJ) to both countries' satisfaction.

Since the 1980s, several small parties have emerged. These include the Innovation and Unity Party (Partido Innovación y Unidad—PINU) and the Christian Democratic Party of Honduras (Partido Demócrata Cristiano de Honduras—PDCH). Both have participated in the national and legislative elections, but neither party has posed a threat to the political domination of the PLH and the PNH. Two newer parties, the Liberty and Refoundation Party (Libertad y Refundación—Libre) and the Anti-Corruption Party (Partido Anticorrupción—PAC), however, have made an impact. After the 2013 election, they held 50 of the 128 seats in the National Congress (37 for Libre and 13 for PAC). While both parties lost ground in the 2017 election, Libre continues to hold 30 seats, making it the second-largest party in the legislature.

As of 2017, there are officially eight political parties represented in the National Congress: the National Party, Liberty and Refoundation, the Liberal Party, the Anti-Corruption Party, the Innovation and Unity Party, the Honduran Patriotic Alliance, the Democratic Unification Party, and the Christian Democratic Party.

THE ROLE OF THE MILITARY

The military was a powerful force in domestic politics beginning in the 1950s. It controlled the presidency from 1963 until 1971. In 1972, the military took power again and kept it another ten years. Today, the National Party has close ties

The first women's group in Honduras was the Women's Cultural Society, formed in 1923. This group fought for economic and political rights for women. But it was not until 1955 that the fight for the right to vote was won. Honduras was the last Latin American country to give women suffrage. Women were also active in the formation of the labor movement and took part in the great banana strike of 1954. By the late 1980s, women were represented at all levels of government, although their numbers were small. Women have held seats in the National Congress and the Supreme Court, high-level executive-branch positions, and mayorships. Both the National Party and the Liberal Party have supported female presidential candidates, and in 2010 María Antonieta de Bográn became the first female vice president.

Women's rights activists have been actively fighting for legislation regarding women's health, economic rights, and the extremely high murder rates and violence suffered by women every day. Women have taken to using social media to tweet at politicians directly while also protesting on the ground. The 2016 murder of environmentalist Berta Cáceres also highlighted the injustices faced by indigenous women and women in poverty. Honduran women are finding their voice, and they are screaming for change.

to the military and has sought military help in tackling the violent gang culture found in many of Honduras's cities, to the point that there are military forces patrolling the streets of cities and towns. The military was also responsible for the 2009 coup against then president Manuel Zelaya.

TODAY'S POLITICS

Forces opposed to Nicaragua's Sandinistas, such as those shown here, used Honduras as a place to train and plan attacks.

The National Party's Juan Orlando Hernández became president in 2014. Hernández won promising a zero-tolerance approach toward organized crime and pledging to bring down the high levels of drug-related violence. His second-term election, however, has created controversy and cast a shadow of doubt and corruption over the legitimacy of his election. Today, Honduran politics is heavily influenced by a variety of special interest groups and political organizations. These groups include business organizations such as

VISITACIÓN PADILLA (1882–1960)

Visitación Padilla was a strong and ambitious woman in Honduras during the early 1900s. She started out as a schoolteacher and soon became Honduras's first female journalist. As a feminist, she was certainly a pioneer in Central America and became the best-known feminist figure in Honduras. She felt it was important to draw women together to fight for what they believed in and what they needed. Padilla became president of the Women's Cultural Society, which led the struggle for women's economic and political rights. She also became involved in heated governmental politics, where she worked for peace during the troubled years of the early twentieth century. In 1924, the United States was planning to send Marines into Honduras to help settle the political problems in Central America. Padilla cofounded the Boletin de Defensa Nacional, which led the protest against US intervention.

A women's group was named the Visitación Padilla Committee in honor of this impressive woman. The committee is dedicated to building a peaceful future for the children of Honduras.

the banana companies, labor and peasant groups—such as the Confederation of Honduran Workers (CTH) and the General Workers Confederation (CGT)—and popular, legally recognized groups—student, women's, human rights, and environmental groups.

INTERNET LINKS

https://www.globalsecurity.org/military/world/centam/ho -political-parties.htm
This website explains the history of political parties in Honduras.

http://www.nationalanthems.info/hn.htm
This website offers a description and history of the national anthem of Honduras.

ECONOMY

A close-up of a lempira, the Honduran currency

4

HONDURAS IS ONE OF THE POOREST developing countries in the Western Hemisphere, and the second poorest country in Central America, with a per head gross domestic product (GDP) of just $5,500 a year in 2017. Hondurans work under difficult conditions for very little income. The economy of Honduras has improved since 2010, but it is still insufficient in improving living standards for the nearly 65 percent of the population in poverty.

The economy is divided geographically between the highlands and the lowlands. The people of the highlands contribute to the nation's economy mainly with subsistence farming, raising livestock, and mining. In the lowlands, the chief occupations are in the plantations. The most important economic centers are San Pedro Sula on the northern coast, which is highly industrialized, and Choluteca on the southern coast, which is a farming center for shrimp, meat, and dairy products.

The political turbulence that plagued Honduras and its Central American neighbors throughout the 1980s and 1990s negatively affected the Honduran economy, which is in need of capital and technical know-how. The economy was also greatly affected by the damage Hurricane Mitch did to important export crops in November 1998. More than 60 percent

Honduran workers carry coffee bean sacks in El Paraíso. Honduras is one of the main producers of the best Arabica coffee in the world.

of that year's fruit crop was destroyed. It took Honduras a decade to rebuild its infrastructure and farming output. In 2004, the United States—Central America Free Trade Agreement (CAFTA) was created to help foster investment from North America. It has meant that Honduran goods can more easily be exported to American markets. However, growth remains dependent on the good health of the US economy, its major trading partner; commodity prices; and international perception of Honduras.

EXPORTS

The economy of Honduras relies on two exports: bananas and coffee. Although Hurricane Mitch virtually wiped out the banana-growing industry in 1998, the industry had recovered to 60 percent of its pre-Mitch levels by 2000. Coffee beans account for over 20 percent of the country's export revenue. As with any developing country that depends on a few exports, the Honduran economy is at the mercy of world prices. However, the government is increasing its involvement in the economy and is diversifying exports in order to develop a more stable economy. In recent years, Honduras has increased exports in apparel and automobile wire harnessing. Beef had the potential to become a very important export in the 1980s. Because of high production costs, the livestock industry now accounts for less than 3 percent of total exports, yet it is still an important export. Honduras also exports cotton, tobacco, pineapples, sugarcane, vegetables, and lobsters and shrimp. The United States is the destination of most Honduran exports.

INDUSTRIES

The Honduran labor force is made up of mainly unskilled and uneducated laborers. More than half the rural population is landless and relies on seasonal labor paying low wages.

The unemployment rate in Honduras is fairly low, at 5.9 percent, but about a third of the population is underemployed, meaning that they are working below their education level or skill.

AGRICULTURE Because of the rugged, mountainous country, only about 15 percent of the land in Honduras can be used for farming, yet agriculture employs 39.2 percent of the labor force and accounts for 13.8 percent of annual GDP. In the highlands and Pacific lowlands, ranching provides employment and livestock products for export. Large agribusinesses take up much of the arable highlands. The rest is divided between subsistence farmers, 55 percent of whom have less than 5 acres (2 hectares) of mediocre farmland and earn less than $2 a day, or $500 per year, from those small plots. Over the past twenty years, the agricultural sector has lost about one-third of its earning power, largely because of a decline in prices for export crops, especially bananas and coffee.

In the Caribbean coastal area, a different type of agriculture is practiced. Two large US companies—Chiquita Brands International (formerly United Fruit Company) and Dole (formerly Standard Fruit and Steamship Company)—hold over half of the arable land. These companies produce a substantial part of the national income growing bananas and coffee beans for export.

FORESTRY Honduras was once famous for its mahogany trees, but now pine is the main commercial forest product. Because Honduras has extensive pine forests, forestry has the potential to contribute a large source of income. However, the country's forests have been heavily exploited and suffered from blight in the 1960s. Large tracts have been cleared for agriculture, especially cattle ranches, and commercial timber exploitation has been inefficient. Many trees felled for lumber do not reach sawmills, and not all that do are processed.

FISHING Though fishing is still a small industry, it is steadily developing along the Caribbean coast. The largest catch is of shrimp, seconded by lobster, most of which is exported to the United States.

MINING Mining produced the main exports in the late 1800s but declined rapidly in importance during the 1900s. The largest mining company, the

Agriculture makes up a major portion of the Honduran economy.

From the late nineteenth to the mid-twentieth century, Honduras's economy was largely dependent upon the production of silver and gold, particularly from the El Mochito mine, which was the largest in Central America at the time. Metals such as zinc, lead, and iron ore have also been found.

New York and Honduras Rosario Mining Company, produced $60 million worth of gold and silver from 1882 to 1954 before discontinuing most of its operations. Mining's contribution to the GDP declined steadily during the 1980s to account for only a tiny percent of the GDP today. Yet Honduras remains the country richest in mineral resources in Central America. Gold, silver, lead, zinc, and cadmium are mined and exported to the United States and Europe, with zinc being the primary mineral export.

Women work in a tobacco processing plant in Honduras.

MANUFACTURING The manufacturing sector employs roughly 20 percent of the workforce and accounts for about 28 percent of GDP. Food, drinks, textiles, clothing, chemicals, lumber, and paper products are the main goods manufactured and processed. Between 1990 and 1998, the number of workers in the sector grew from 9,000 to 120,000. A majority of these workers—70 percent—were women between the ages of fifteen and twenty-six. Industrial plants are located largely in the urban areas of San Pedro Sula and Tegucigalpa. Manufacturing has attracted more foreign investment than any other industry in Honduras. Small Honduran shops make mostly clothing and food products, while Asian-owned textile industries have begun to dominate the smaller domestic manufacturing economy.

SERVICES Roughly 40 percent of the population of Honduras works in the service industry (including transportation and tourism). Services make up 57.8 percent of the country's income. Many Hondurans work as domestic help in the cities.

In the mid-1990s, financial services in Honduras were opened up, and the banking industry expanded rapidly. By the early part of the twenty-first century, financial assets in Honduras had been consolidated into the hands of a few large banks.

TOURISM Tourism is one of the fastest-growing industries in Honduras. There are many beautiful natural attractions, most of them pristine and unspoiled. Travelers come to Honduras to visit the Mayan ruins in Copán and the outstanding coral reef off the Bay Islands. Small ecotourism projects are considered to have significant potential, especially in the Bay Islands. The number of tourist arrivals in Honduras was reported at 880,000 in 2015. In the following year, tourism earned the country $686 million (up from $567 million in 2007).

Tourists hike to visit Pulhapanzak Waterfall.

ENERGY

For many years, Hondurans have relied on fuelwood and biomass, mostly waste products from agricultural production, to supply them with energy. These sources have met approximately 50 percent of the country's total energy demand. Hydroelectric plants where rivers have been dammed provide about a quarter of Honduras's electricity. Honduran use of electricity is low but increasing. In urban areas, approximately 97 percent of the people have access to electricity, but in rural areas about 66 percent of the people have access. While the numbers are getting better, about nine hundred thousand people are still without access to electricity. Petroleum has never been produced in Honduras, so the country has relied on oil imports to fill much of its energy needs. A significant part of total export earnings are spent on purchasing oil.

TELECOMMUNICATIONS

Historically the telecommunications system in Honduras was outdated and poorly maintained. However, this has improved during the past decade. As of 2016, there were 442,929 fixed telephone lines in use across the country (roughly 5 per 100 people). Half the phones are in Tegucigalpa, a quarter are in San Pedro Sula, and the remainder are scattered all over the country in large towns. However, almost 8 million Hondurans have cellular phones, or

The Feria Centroamericana de Turismo y Artesanía, a Central American international tourism and crafts fair, is held annually from December 6 to 16 in Tegucigalpa.

A group of Hondurans watch the news following the coup against President Zelaya.

roughly 88 percent of the population, as this is the cheapest and easiest way to make phone calls. As of 2016, internet use has grown to 2,667,978 users, as compared with 424,200 users recorded in 2007.

Television is popular; there are now thirty-nine channels. The television channels in Honduras broadcast news, *novelas* (soap operas), variety shows, movies, sports, and entertainment. Stations with daily news reports about Honduras are broadcast almost exclusively in Spanish. Radio is a major mode of getting information to Hondurans. All parts of the country are in the range of at least one radio station.

TRANSPORTATION

Because of the mountainous terrain, it has been difficult to create a transportation system to meet the entire country's needs. In 2012, Honduras had 9,160 miles (14,742 km) of roads, only 2,092 miles (3,367 km) of which were paved. Most of these roads connect the ports and industrial areas. Only one paved highway joins the Caribbean and the Pacific, passing through Puerto Cortés, San Pedro Sula, and Tegucigalpa. This major highway was badly damaged by Hurricane Mitch in November 1998, but it was the first road to be rebuilt. The Inter-American Highway (part of the Pan-American Highway) cuts across southern Honduras for about 100 miles (160 km). Other areas, served only by gravel and dirt roads that are often impassable during even moderately rainy weather, were accessible only by air after the hurricane.

The railroads were built by the original banana companies for transporting bananas to ports, not for transporting goods and passengers nationwide. Two rail systems provide freight and passenger service, and both are located in the north-central and northwestern coastal areas. Tegucigalpa remains the only Spanish-speaking capital in the Americas with no rail service whatsoever.

Four ports handle Honduras's seaborne trade—Puerto Cortés, Tela, La Ceiba, and Puerto Castilla. Most of the agricultural exports and imports of petroleum and manufactured products pass through Puerto Cortés.

Lack of alternative transportation through Honduras's mountains makes air travel important. There are four international airports—in Tegucigalpa, La Ceiba, Roatán, and near San Pedro Sula. Domestic flights operate between the cities and to Roatán. There is also air service to rural areas where planes land on small, unpaved fields.

WAGES

Each industry has its own minimum wage based on an eight-hour day shift. Overtime is paid for a shift of over eight hours, and the rate is higher if overtime hours occur during the night or are an extension of the night shift

In 2008, President Manuel Zelaya increased the minimum wage by 60 percent, raising monthly wages from $181 to $289. As of 2016, the minimum wage now ranges from 5,681.73 lempiras ($240.24) to 8,803.70 lempiras ($372.25) per month, depending on the industry. Although the new minimum wage was welcomed by many, some businesses have struggled to pay the higher costs, and workers have been laid off as a consequence.

A customer speaks with a cashier in a clothing store in Tegucigalpa. Retail stores such as this one are common in the larger cities in Honduras.

INTERNET LINKS

https://www.hondurastravel.com/honduras-history/ferrocarril-nacional-de-honduras
This website delves into the historic railroads in Honduras.

https://www.roatanet.com/roatan-in-tv-shows-and-movies
This website explores the Honduran film/television and tourism industries.

http://www.worldstopexports.com/honduras-top-10-exports
This website offers a more in-depth look at Honduras's exports.

ENVIRONMENT

A once heavily wooded forest of mahogany trees has been overly logged for the lumber.

5

H ONDURAS HAS AN EXTREMELY diverse environmental landscape, spanning beaches, rain forests, valleys, and mountains. With so many different habitats, Honduras has a unique variety of wildlife, such that there are conservation efforts under way to save the endangered species of the region. There is such an abundance of both flora and fauna that Honduras is considered a biodiversity "hotspot."

Today, the country's main environmental issues are deforestation and soil erosion, both consequences of mining, logging, and land cultivation for farming. In recent years, the Honduran government has sought to introduce pro-environmental legislation, but the biggest challenge is to help poor subsistence farmers exploit the forest in a responsible way. Pesticides used by banana producers have also produced environmental damage along the coastlines. Although 75 percent of Honduras's rain forest is under government management, the government lacks funds to effectively manage the forest, and parks are understaffed.

ILLEGAL LOGGING AND DEFORESTATION

About 45 percent of Honduras—19,575 square miles (50,700 sq km)—is covered in forest. It is home to many species of animals. There are

Honduras has a number of thriving local conservation organizations. The Honduran Conservation Coalition was established in 2011 and is a network of conservationists and scientists that promotes citizen science, community-based conservation, and environmentally friendly sustainable development in Honduras and elsewhere in Mesoamerica.

Leaded gasoline, which causes air pollution, has been phased out in Honduras. However, for many years, the law was ignored by most Hondurans, and the authorities rarely prosecuted vehicles that used leaded gas. In recent years, the government has sought to clamp down on leaded gasoline use, to a great extent because of pressure from local environmental activists.

many protected biosphere reserves and national parks. Moskitia—the Mosquito Coast—is one of Central America's few remaining areas of untamed wilderness. Huge expanses of untouched jungle are inhabited by small numbers of indigenous people, living a traditional lifestyle that has not changed in centuries. The area is home to a vast array of wildlife, including manatees, tapirs, crocodiles, toucans, macaws, and herons. However, in the Moskitia region, the Río Plátano Biosphere Reserve has suffered huge damage to its forests due to increased farming and logging of its resources.

Illegal logging is the main cause of deforestation in Honduras. By some estimates, as much as 85 percent of timber is harvested illegally. According to a 2005 investigation, the illegal timber trade feeds corruption among local government officials, politicians, police, and businesspeople, since so many people profit from the logging. According to some environmental organizations, Honduras suffered the greatest percentage loss of forest cover of any Latin American country at the end of the twentieth century. Between 1990 and 2005, 37 percent of the country's forests disappeared, at a rate of more than 252,400 acres (102,143 ha) per year.

To a great degree, Honduras's rapid deforestation is caused by the country's debilitating poverty, with poor subsistence farmers clearing forest to graze cattle and raise crops. Wood is also gathered for fuel (50 percent of the country's energy comes from fuelwood) or to sell as timber. As recently as 2016, Honduras was in negotiations with the European Union to not only help tackle illegal logging but also to drive sustainable development.

Forestry provides jobs for many thousands of Hondurans, and in a country where most of the population lives in poverty, the environment will always come second to people's livelihood. Increased government enforcement of logging laws is helping to limit the tree loss, but deforestation continues to deplete the country's forests.

Deforestation can also make the likelihood of mudslides much greater, as natural vegetation anchors the soil and reduces the amount of earth that can be easily washed away by rains and floods. Aerial surveys following Hurricane Mitch suggested that mudslides were worst in deforested areas.

Various hydroelectric projects have been planned in Honduras as a way of harnessing the power of the country's many mountain rivers and improving its inefficient energy supply. One project, a series of three dams on the Patuca River, is still in progress. Conservationists warned that the dams would do untold damage to local protected rain forests, including the Patuca National Park, the Tawhaka Asangni Biosphere Reserve, and the Río Plátano Biosphere Reserve, and the project was abandoned in the late 1990s. However, it was restarted in 2007, to the dismay of river conservationists. The first of the three dams was expected to be finished in 2018.

Mangrove trees have an extensive network of roots, as can be seen here on this mangrove tree off the coast of Roatán.

MANGROVES

Honduras has more native mangrove forest than any other country in Central America. Mangrove forests stabilize the coastline, reducing erosion from storm surges, currents, waves, and tides. The intricate root system of mangroves also makes these forests attractive to fish and other organisms seeking food and shelter from predators. The Honduran mangroves, which are found on both the Caribbean and Pacific coasts, are threatened with destruction by the shrimp industry, deforestation, and unsustainable building development. Local and international environmental groups are seeking to protect the environment of one of the largest areas of mangroves, the Gulf of Fonseca, by educating local fishermen to take advantage of the gulf's resources without harming the environment. By some estimates, the Gulf of Fonseca has lost about 40 percent of its original mangrove forests.

ENDANGERED AND VULNERABLE ANIMALS

The International Union for Conservation of Nature (IUCN) lists three species of mammal as endangered and four others as vulnerable in Honduras. The Baird's tapir, Geoffroy spider monkey, and Roatán Island agouti are considered endangered. The country's national bird, the scarlet macaw (a type of parrot), was on the endangered list for quite some time, but it is currently stable due to conservation efforts. The main threat to the animals is deforestation.

The wildlife refuges of Punta Sal and the Laguna de Micos on the northern Caribbean coast are breeding grounds for shrimp, crabs, many types of fish, manatees, and dolphins. However, this makes them attractive to local fishermen, who have flouted the law in search of fish. The use of nets for fishing in rivers, estuaries, and the sea poses a particular threat to manatees. Recently, manatee numbers have risen, but they are still listed as a threatened species.

The Baird's tapir is native to Honduras and is currently an endangered species. Conservation efforts are being made to protect and encourage the growth of the population.

CLOUD FORESTS

As a mountainous land, Honduras has more "cloud forests" than any other Central American country. Cloud forests are areas of tropical forest at high altitude. Many of Honduras's national parks include highland cloud forests. Cloud forests form a remarkable and unique ecosystem. At altitudes of 5,905 feet (1,800 m) or more, the clouds deposit tiny drops of water on the forest trees and plants, beginning a process called "'horizontal precipitation." Unlike lowland jungle, plants like bromeliads, orchids, clusia trees, and tree ferns can grow in cloud forests. Many mosses and other fungi also thrive in the cooler, damp climate of these high-altitude forests. Although highly elusive, one of the most attractive residents of the cloud forest is the quetzal bird. There are large populations of this beautiful bird in Cusuco National Park, Pico Pujol, Sierra de Agalta, and La Muralla National Park. The cloud forests are also home to the blue morpho butterfly, cougars, tapirs, sloths, and many species of monkeys.

NATIONAL PARKS AND RESERVES

Honduras has many protected areas and nature reserves, including government-managed national parks, biosphere reserves, and wildlife refuges. More than a fifth of the country is designated reserve status. Some of the most important protected areas include the following.

The mining ghost town of San Juancito is located in La Tigra National Park.

LA TIGRA NATIONAL PARK As the first national park of the country, La Tigra National Park is a popular destination for day-trippers from Tegucigalpa. It is a cloud forest preserve for a large variety of plant and animal life. The park's moss-covered world of trees laden with bromeliads, orchids, and ferns lends a feeling of mystery. The many mammals include tapirs, monkeys, and the rarely seen ocelot and jaguar. The park is also home to many colorful birds, including the resplendent quetzal, the emerald toucan, and the cinnamon-bellied flower-piercer. Visitors to La Tigra can hike miles of well-maintained, well-marked trails past a scenic waterfall and an abandoned silver mine or traverse the length of the park via a lookout point with an impressive view of Tegucigalpa.

CUERO Y SALADO WILDLIFE REFUGE Covering 33,000 acres (13,255 ha) and situated on the coast near La Ceiba, the reserve is named after the two local rivers, Cuero and Salado, that meet to form a large estuary. The park is home to rarely seen manatees, as well as howler and white-faced monkeys, sloths, agoutis, iguanas, and hundreds of bird species.

LANCETILLA BOTANICAL GARDENS Covering about 4,150 acres (1,680 ha), this is the only botanical garden in Honduras and the second-largest botanical garden in the world. The gardens were established in 1926 by the Tela Railroad Company to experiment with growing various types of tropical plants. The gardens are home to numerous species of birds and the largest single collection of tropical fruit trees in the Western Hemisphere. Many rare animals have also made their home here, such as the puma, howler monkey, wildcat, and deer.

LAGUNA DE BACALAR In 2003, this marine coastal wetland of 18,271 acres (7,394 ha) was designated as a Wetland of International Importance. Located on the Caribbean coast, this marine wetland is characterized by broad-leaf forest, swamps, and mangrove forest. The area is also home to endangered species such as the Caribbean manatee, rare birds such as the jabiru, and fish typical of this type of ecosystem, including the schoolmaster snapper and the horse-eye jack.

THE RÍO PLÁTANO BIOSPHERE RESERVE This United Nations Educational, Scientific and Cultural Organization (UNESCO) World Heritage site is located in the region of Moskitia. At 1.3 million acres (525,000 ha), it is the largest park in Honduras. The reserve is an extremely diverse biosphere that includes lagoons, coastal beaches, marshes, and pine forests. Animals that have made their home here include the green iguana, sea turtles, white-tailed deer, and red deer.

SANITATION

Although the water supply and sanitation has improved during the past decade, much of Honduras's sewage system is unreliable. Some rural areas still do not have any proper water supply, with villagers collecting water from local rivers, springs, and wells. Much of the water and sewage system was destroyed by Hurricane Mitch, and it has taken many years to repair the damage. Although the Honduran authorities have sought to improve the country's sewage system, there is little money available for such an expensive project. Honduras is not fully exploiting its water resources and is using only a fraction of the potential water available.

Water quality in Honduras is poor by Latin American standards. In 2006, only 75 percent of the drinking water in urban areas was disinfected and 10 percent of the sewage received treatment. In rural areas, the service was worse, with only a third of drinking water being treated. According to the WHO, most homes receive intermittent water supplies for an average of only

Hondurans from the city of Tegucigalpa bring clean drinking water to a smaller community just north of the city.

six hours a day. However, improvements have been made in recent years. In 2015, 91 percent of the total population had access to improved water and 83 percent of the total population had access to improved sanitation.

Due to a drought exacerbated by El Niño, Honduras declared a national emergency in 2015. People were forced to start migrating to find work to be able to pay for food. Approximately 170,000 children under age five were facing malnutrition and disease due to the lack of clean water in Honduras. Community volunteers, health staff, church leaders, and sanitation committees have responded by partnering with nonprofit organizations to train families on treating water and practicing basic sanitation.

The quality of drinking water and inefficient sanitation is also a cause of disease and illness in Honduras, especially in rural areas. The rapid increase of the urban poor, as many Hondurans move from the villages to the towns and cities for work, has also put extra strain on urban sewage systems. Waterborne diseases such as hepatitis A and typhoid are still common in Honduras.

WATER POLLUTION

Honduras's coastal mangroves and reed beds, waters, and reefs have become affected by pollution, especially in recent years. The main causes of pollution in the marine environment are overfishing, poor sewage management, and pesticide run-off from farming. The coastal areas have also been put under tremendous pressure by the development of tourist facilities for the growing tourism industry.

The vast Mesoamerican barrier reef system runs off Honduras's Caribbean coast, close to the Bay Islands. It is part of the second-largest coral reef in the world, stretching from Honduras up to the Yucatán Peninsula in Mexico, and it is home to many important marine species. Tourism, fishing, and cargo ship traffic have all contributed to damaging the reef. However, local environmental groups, such as the Bay Islands Conservation Association, are working to protect and restore the reef. Based on methods tested in the Pacific, dying corals are planted and regenerated. Conservationists in the Bay Islands have also sought to nurture the local turtle population by protecting their nesting grounds. Turtles visit the islands every year from May until the end of October.

Mining has also caused water pollution in Honduras. The San Martin gold mine in the central Siria Valley region was first opened in 1999. Cyanide has been used there to extract the gold ore through "heap leaching," a method that percolates and separates the gold from the other metals. It is one of the cheapest and quickest ways to extract gold ore. However, local people complained that the cyanide and arsenic polluted their water supplies. In 2007, the mining company was fined by the government and ordered to mine in a way that complied with environmental regulations. The San Martin gold mine is now closed due to the severe pollution and damage to the surrounding villages it caused.

INTERNET LINKS

http://bayislandsconservationassociation.org
Visit the Bay Island Conservation Association website to learn about and protect the Bay Islands' natural resources.

https://europa.eu/capacity4dev/article/eu-honduras-timber -negotiations-strengthen-fight-against-illegal-logging
This site offers information on illegal logging in Honduras and negotiations on how to stop it.

https://www.honduranconservationcoalition.com
The Honduras Conservation Coalition website provides information on its conservation efforts.

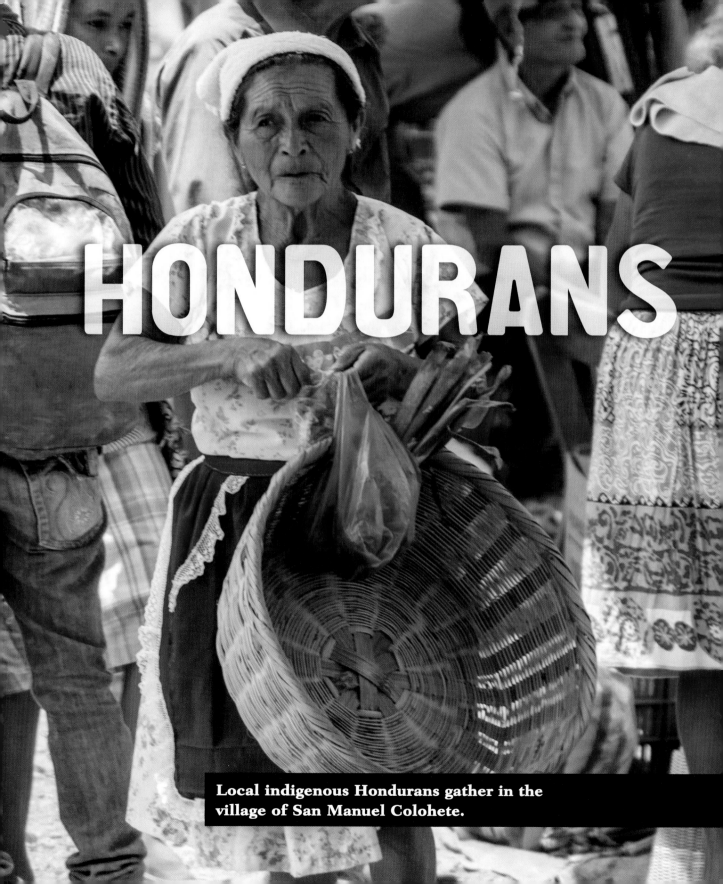

HONDURANS

Local indigenous Hondurans gather in the village of San Manuel Colohete.

THE POPULATION OF HONDURAS IS A mix of different cultures and peoples that have come together through a long history of migration, colonization, and a common locale. In recent years, people have started to move from the rural mountains into the big cities. As of 2017, the population was estimated to be over nine million. Approximately 56 percent of the people live in the cities. About 90 percent of the population is mestizo, people who are a racial mix of indigenous and European ancestry. The remaining inhabitants include indigenous peoples (7 percent), blacks from Africa and the Caribbean Islands (2 percent), whites who come mostly from Europe (1 percent), and a small number of immigrants from the Middle East.

6

According to a 2017 estimate, the median age of Hondurans was just twenty-three years old, meaning that the country has a very young population, with many more young people than elderly people.

THE LADINO PEOPLE

Mestizos, whites, and most blacks are Ladino—people who speak Spanish and whose lifestyle follows Hispanic cultural patterns. Most Ladinos are members of the Roman Catholic Church. They range from poor subsistence farmers to businesspeople in the cities. Family is at the core of Ladino culture. These close family connections make it difficult for immigrants to penetrate Ladino culture, so different and separate subcultures of immigrants exist in the cities of Honduras. This lack of ethnic mixing may seem surprising because almost all Ladinos themselves have a mixed racial ancestry. It is not that they are unfriendly, but that Ladinos simply value their extended families above all else, and so they remain in tight-knit groups.

—An indigenous Honduran woman stands outside of a traditional home.

INDIGENOUS TRIBES

Since colonial times, there has been intermarriage between the Native Hondurans and Spanish people. The remaining indigenous population consists of many different small groups who maintain customs set apart from Ladino culture.

THE LENCA One of the largest remaining indigenous groups in Honduras is the Lenca, who are believed to have descended from the ancient Maya. Estimates suggest that there are up to one hundred thousand Lenca, living mainly in the southwestern interior. Lenca women buy and sell vegetables in a market at La Esperanza-Intibucá and in Marcala.

The Lenca still practice some traditional customs. They cultivate communal lands instead of owning private plots, and they use digging sticks instead of plows. Women wear long skirts and short blouses similar to those worn by women in colonial days. They usually work alongside the men in the fields. Other characteristics that set the Lenca apart are their festival dances, basket-weaving, pottery, and home brewing of the traditional liquor, chicha.

They have adopted some aspects of the Ladino national culture. The Lenca are Catholic, although they are more religious than the average Ladino, and they no longer speak their native language but instead speak dialects that have borrowed Spanish words. For these reasons, there has been some debate as to whether the Lenca can be considered truly indigenous.

THE CHORTÍ The Chortí are another group with Mayan heritage. They live mostly near the town of Copán. Chortí villagers grow crops and trade in handicrafts. They are skilled makers of woven baskets, pottery, soap, wooden products, and leather goods.

THE JICAQUE In the past, northern indigenous groups were less settled than those living in the mountainous southwest. These groups were basically hunters and fishers. One northern group, the Jicaque (numbering roughly 8,600), once lived on the Caribbean coast until they were driven inland by colonists, where they began to settle and cultivate corn like the western tribes. Only a few hundred maintain their language and traditions. They dress in old-style tunics. Their homes are distinctive, made of planks tied with vines and roofed with thatch. They still hunt with blowguns.

THE MISKITO The Miskito people are an isolated group who live harmoniously on the Mosquito Coast in northeastern Honduras. The area was essentially ignored by the Spanish, so the Miskito were left to themselves, more so than the rest of the indigenous people of Honduras. They number approximately forty thousand people.

There has been intermarriage between the Miskito and blacks, often escaped slaves who sought the north coast for refuge. The Miskito today are a racially mixed population of indigenous, African, and European origin, mostly British. Many still speak a Creole language with contributions from Spanish, English, and German. They are generally considered indigenous.

Miskito cultivate yucca, beans, and corn in shifting agriculture. They burn and clear plots, then move on when the land is exhausted, leaving it to replenish itself. They also raise livestock such as chickens, pigs, and cows.

Because the Miskito live on the coast and rely on waterways for transportation, they have developed their own style of dugout and flat-bottom boats. Fishing is important to their livelihood. Some Miskito stun their catch with arrows poisoned with an extract from jungle vines.

THE CHOROTEGA, PIPIL, PAYA, AND PECH These other indigenous groups number only a couple of hundred people. The Chorotega migrated from Mexico in pre-Columbian times and have retained many of their religious and cultural traits. The Pipil, who are of Nahuatl descent, live along the southwestern mountain slopes.

The exact origin of the Paya is unknown, but their ancestors are believed to have come from South America. They live in the lush and humid river regions of the Mosquito Coast, many near the Río Plátano, working as subsistence farmers and fishermen. They use farming tools, fishing poles, and spears that they make themselves.

The Pech, another indigenous group of the Mosquito Coast, are believed to be descendants of the Paya. Today their population has been reduced to fewer than 2,500. The Pech men fish, and women tend to crops and livestock. Pech children now go to Pech schools during the day but still help their parents before and after school.

AFRO-HONDURANS

There are two distinct groups of Afro-Hondurans: the Black Carib, known as the Garifuna, and the black population in the Bay Islands.

The Black Carib settled in coastal villages along the Caribbean in the early 1800s. They are descendants of freed African slaves who were deported by the British in 1797 from the island of Saint Vincent in the Caribbean. They speak a Carib-based Creole that mixes English with local languages. The Black Carib people share many customs with the Miskito. Both groups have been self-sufficient through farming and fishing for generations, but today, many of the men have to work outside the region to supplement an income that has been reduced by a loss of land. Many families are split up for long periods of time.

Many of the population on the Bay Islands are of mixed race. These people have descended from English-speaking Africans and whites from Belize and the Cayman Islands. Their traditions are distinctly West Indian, and they speak Creole or Caribbean English.

ARAB HONDURANS

There is a thriving Arab community in Honduras descended from immigrants who arrived in the early 1900s, mostly from Palestine and Lebanon. The Arabs have remained culturally distinct by keeping many of their own traditions alive. They were first successful as merchants and then moved to the industrial cities where they have become economically quite powerful.

Young Garifuna men play music on the beach at Chachauate in the Cayos Cochinos Islands in Honduras.

WEALTH DISPARITY AND SOCIAL CLASS

Honduras is one of the poorest countries in the Western Hemisphere, with wealth very unevenly spread: the top 10 percent of the population controls nearly 40 percent of the country's wealth. The majority of Hondurans are poverty-stricken subsistence farmers, hired hands on large corporate farms, or poorly paid laborers in the cities. Since the 1950s, however, a small middle class has also emerged. There is little social conflict between the classes, but the increasing poverty of the majority and an increase in the wealth and power of the upper class has long been a concern.

THE ELITE The Honduran elite is divided into two basic groups—the traditional elite, who were originally owners of large rural estates, and the military elite. The traditional elite were *hacendados* (hah-sen-DAH-dohs), the owners of large haciendas in the interior highlands and valleys. Many still live on their estates. After World War II, this group of wealthy landowners became involved in cattle production in response to the increase in the beef market. However, the land they used for cattle ranching—ultimately to export food to other countries—had originally been used for domestic food production. Therefore,

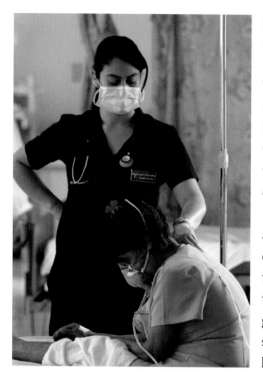

A Honduran doctor checks her patient at the Torax Hospital in Tegucigalpa.

social tensions increased in rural Honduras between the upper and lower classes.

This group of wealthy people is not particularly cohesive. They have different interests when it comes to political and economic issues. Many of them also have competing businesses. Politically there are as many conservatives as there are liberals. Some liberals support and work toward the social change that middle and lower classes have sought over the years.

The military elite emerged in the mid-1950s when the armed forces underwent a major transformation. The military developed from being a variety of provincial militia groups to a United States—trained national institution. Because the traditional elite did not favor this military institution, the two groups have remained distinct. Possibly as a result of this separation of interest between the two elite groups, neither has become overwhelmingly powerful.

THE MIDDLE CLASS The small group that makes up the middle class is growing at a steady pace and is mostly settled in the cities. People who are considered middle class are those with a higher education—college students, professors, teachers, civil servants, engineers, and merchants. On the Caribbean coast, the growth of the middle class was directly related to the area's industrial and business enterprises. In the north, the success of merchants was due to the market demands created by employed workers in the area's agribusiness. Although the middle class makes a decent income compared with the lower class, their income is still low by North American standards.

This group is still small because although the growth in industry and commerce has improved in the last decade, it has still been slow by world standards, and over a third of the population is underemployed. Job opportunities are scarce, but many people move to the cities every year seeking to end their poverty and live a middle-class lifestyle. Many middle-class citizens are involved in the politics of social change. They create and join unions, church groups, and other political organizations.

THE LOWER CLASS The lower class is divided into two groups based on where they live. Traditionally, the poor people of Honduras have been the peasants in rural areas, but there is a growing lower class in the cities. Peasants are subsistence farmers called *campesinos* who make a living off their land.

Today, because so much land has been absorbed by commercial agribusiness, family subsistence off the land is difficult. This situation began after the 1950s, when cattle and cotton production for export increased and land was absorbed to become part of large agribusinesses. When the small plots of land were no longer enough to support the family, people either went to work on nearby large farms or migrated to the cities in search of employment.

The urban poor now consists of many of the campesinos who moved to cities looking for employment opportunities. This has created a very large population of impoverished, unemployed people looking for work and living on the streets in cities such as Tegucigalpa and San Pedro Sula. Many of those

Extreme poverty plagues Honduras. Honduras is ranked as one of the poorest nations in the Western Hemisphere.

Most towns have folk dance groups that wear traditional dress. A common style, originally worn by the Lenca, is all white for men and women. The white, flowing cotton material called manta *was once worn mainly by the poor, but its use has spread widely. This style of dress is considered most appropriate for dancing Lenca and mestizo dances with indigenous influences. It is also the most common clothing for dolls made in the central region. Another very popular folk dance dress is that found in the La Paz department. Women's dresses are very brightly colored and often have shiny metallic decorations or colored ribbons that flutter as the women dance.*

who do find work end up employed in the service industry, doing domestic work such as cleaning the homes of the wealthy. Some join the construction industry, while others join the assembly lines that manufacture products such as shoes, clothing, baskets, and furniture.

DEMOGRAPHIC CHANGES

In the second half of the twentieth century, there has been a major increase in the population, but the population density is still relatively low. Fertility rates are high by standards in developed countries, but they have gone down in recent years, reaching 2.67 children born per woman in 2017. Significant immigration from neighboring Central American countries has led to higher levels of civil conflict.

The growth of the banana industry resulted in the first major shift in population. In the early 1900s, many Hondurans moved to the Caribbean coast to seek employment on the plantations. Today, most internal migration is from rural areas to urban centers, especially the two largest cities, Tegucigalpa and San Pedro Sula. In the 1950s, Tegucigalpa's population increased by 75 percent, causing inadequate housing and the emergence of shantytowns. As of 2018, the population of the capital was about 1.3 million.

Most migrants today are in their teens or early twenties, and they seek a better standard of living beyond the poverty of farm life. This makes sense when looking at the population distribution, as the majority of the population falls into this age group. Honduran men tend to move from their family land to wherever there is a developing agricultural area or to cities for work in artisan shops or as laborers in factories or construction. Women, on the other hand, have a limited choice when it comes to employment. Most migrant women are those who want to escape economic hardship, early marriage, and motherhood. These women end up in the cities working as domestic help for the elite, in factories, or as street vendors.

STYLE OF DRESS

Hondurans value physical appearance, and they dress formally, conservatively, and neatly. Ladinos wear Western-style clothes. Women usually wear a colorful dress or a skirt and blouse, while men wear long-sleeved dress shirts and slacks. Wearing jeans with a T-shirt is considered too informal, especially outdoors in Tegucigalpa or San Pedro Sula. Children always wear uniforms to school. Children in public schools wear white and blue. Private schools have their own colored uniforms. The cities can look very colorful when school lets out, with all the children wearing clothing of various colors.

Indigenous groups each have their own traditional dress. They wear clothing that varies from completely traditional dress to a mixture of Western and traditional styles.

A well-dressed, indigenous Honduran man uses his cell phone in San Manuel Colohete, Honduras.

INTERNET LINKS

http://minorityrights.org/country/honduras
This page offers further information on the indigenous groups of Honduras.

http://traveltips.usatoday.com/type-clothing-people-honduras -wear-64073.html
This site offers a breakdown of the different clothing worn in Honduras.

LIFESTYLE

Cobblestone streets line the village of Copán Ruinas.

HONDURAS HAS TRADITIONALLY been a farming society, and in spite of recent urban growth, it is still one of the least urbanized countries of Central America. The poor rural living conditions are of special concern, as the people are malnourished and are perpetually struggling to make ends meet.

In 1990, roughly 44 percent of Hondurans lived in towns and cities. In 2017, the number reached 56 percent. This rapid move from the country to the towns and cities has placed great pressure on Hondurans' traditional sense of community, with greater numbers of people competing for fewer jobs. Yet families provide an important support system that keeps Hondurans relatively content by helping one another and creating a real sense of community.

FAMILY TIES

The family is the cornerstone of Honduran society and culture. Extended families are close-knit, often living in one home including not only grandparents but also aunts, uncles, and cousins. The closest relationships are usually familial ones, and any leisure time, such as celebrating festivals, is spent with relatives. Children are taught from a young age that relatives are to be trusted above everyone else. Families provide important social support, especially for women. And when men go into business, it is usually with other family members.

7

Thousands of Hondurans—especially young men—leave the country each year, most of them to find better-paid work in the United States. The money sent home by the overseas workers is an important source of income for many families.

Men and women often taken on traditional roles in Honduran families.

A discrepancy exists, however, between this ideal of family and some Honduran families. Marriage is expensive, so many couples live together but are not legally married. Many men abandon their wives, girlfriends, and children, especially in the cities. Many households are run by single mothers, especially in Tegucigalpa. Honduran society disapproves of a man who does not support his children. Despite this, some men do not assume the responsibilities of fatherhood.

MEN'S ROLES The concept of machismo is evident throughout all socioeconomic levels. Men are expected to be macho—daring, strong, unemotional, and brave. Men prove their masculinity or machismo by flirting with women, being demanding, and acting in an aggressive way. Boys are encouraged from an early age to act freely, and they mostly do not help out around the house. Effeminate behavior is usually ridiculed in a country where macho values hold sway.

The father's role varies depending on the family, but generally fathers must be respected and obeyed. They are more removed from daily family affairs but usually have the final say in important matters. Men often do not feel a responsibility for their children, expecting women to take care of them completely. Men run the farms or send money home if they are working elsewhere.

WOMEN'S ROLES The female ideal of *marianismo* (mah-ree-ahn-EEZ-moh) is to be loyal, chaste, and submissive. Girls are encouraged to be more emotional and more vulnerable. Women are supposed to take care of their husbands or boyfriends and their children. However, Honduran women are strong and capable. They often work in the fields alongside men, in addition to working in the kitchen.

More women are getting a higher education today, but those who do are still paid less than men for the same kind of work. Grandmothers and aunts often take care of the children so that a young mother can work outside the home or go to school.

CHILDREN Children are valued, honored, and cherished. They are expected to work hard at home and at school, but they are pampered as well. Generally speaking, children are valued as the next generation, and parents want their children to be better educated and have more money than they did.

Schoolchildren line up at a school in the Honduran village of San Ramón.

However, this ideal is not completely followed in poverty-stricken families. Children of such families are often not pampered at all, and they are sometimes ignored. Men who permanently leave their families often do not send money to their wives or girlfriends in order to provide for their children. When a woman has children from a previous relationship, they may not be cared for by her new husband or boyfriend, as they are not his own.

Young boys and girls are treated very differently. Boys can run around unsupervised, while girls are expected to be quiet and helpful. These attributes fall within the ideals of machismo and marianismo. Girls are carefully groomed and chaperoned, and are vigilantly guarded against immoral conduct.

ELDERS Grandparents almost always live with their families. They are held in high regard and are viewed as a source of wisdom. They are treated and spoken to with the utmost respect. However, grandparents rarely get very old, unless they come from a wealthy family, due to the lack of proper food and health care. Poverty and old age are rarely seen together, and elders work as long as they are able. For them, there is no such thing as retirement.

CHILDBIRTH

Women accept pregnancies with joy, even though they may not be able to afford to have children. Women in rural areas do not have hospitals to go to for childbirth, so birthing takes place at home with the help of the town's midwife, or simply other women in the family. Godparents are chosen and children are baptized in a Catholic church as soon as a priest is in town, which may not be until the next festival. If this is the case, many babies are baptized on the same day, and a large town party may follow afterward. The godparents are generally closely trusted friends, and it is seen as a great honor to be chosen.

COURTSHIP AND MARRIAGE

It is taboo for two teenagers to go on a date without a chaperone. If a date is arranged, sometimes the girl's whole family will go along. In this case, the boyfriend is expected to pay for the whole family. Because of widespread poverty, young Hondurans cannot afford to date often, and marriages often take place after very little courtship.

Marriages, especially in rural areas, are often common-law because religious marriages are expensive and there may not be a residential priest. Some couples get a civil marriage, which is less expensive and makes it easier to get a divorce should things not work out. Middle- and upper-class couples usually have religious marriages with a formal engagement.

DEATH

A Catholic funeral is very important in Honduras. The funeral service in church is followed by nine days of mourning at the deceased person's home. This practice is repeated on the death anniversary.

RURAL LIFE

For campesinos, or peasants, who live in the mountains, work is difficult and is never over. But no matter how busy or tired they are, rural people are often smiling and laughing at stories they share with one another. If they need to travel somewhere, such as the market, they go on foot, often spending the greatest part of their day walking.

A campesina wakes up at 5:00 a.m. and begins work in the kitchen. If she has daughters, they will get up and help too. Women spend the day making tortillas for their families. They boil, wash, and grind the corn to make coarse corn flour. They also bake bread, preserve fruit, wash clothes by hand, clean the house, and feed the chickens and cows. Mothers of infants tend to the babies, while older girls spend much of their time looking after younger siblings.

Campesinos often wake up as early as 3:00 a.m. with their sons. They head out to the fields to plant, tend crops, or harvest. They use hoes, machetes, and digging sticks, and carry loads such as sacks of seed on their backs. Boys will receive their own plot of land to be responsible for at a young age. Children often have the job of scaring birds from cornfields with slingshots, fetching water, and carrying a hot lunch from home to their fathers and older brothers in the field.

Farmers use the traditional slash-and-burn method. Every two years, families move to a new plot of land when the soil they have been farming has lost all its nutrients. They clear the land by slashing the growth down to the ground, then burning away the rest. Today, farmers are being taught soil conservation techniques such as terracing so that they will be able to farm one piece of land much longer.

Some campesinos also spend a part of their week squeezing sugarcane for juice to make sugar blocks to sell. Many campesinos are forced to find part-time work away from home to supplement their incomes, as there is not enough land for all of them.

Two Honduran fathers work on a farm to provide food for their families.

MARKETS Some families spend much of their time growing or making things to sell at the market. The families that do not live in a town with a market will load a small cart with their merchandise, which is then pulled by the family cow. Hondurans may walk up to 20 miles (32 km) over mountain ranges without any paths to get to a market. At the market, some women carry handmade baskets filled with flat breads on their heads as they look for buyers. Men and women work stalls where people come to barter over merchandise. They sell vegetables, fruit, bread, and chickens, as well as handmade straw hats, baskets, wooden statues of saints, vases, and toys.

DWELLINGS Families often live in tiny rural towns, sometimes as small as a dozen dwellings clustered near a rundown church, which often doubles as a one-

In the 1980s and 1990s, when Honduras and its neighbors were involved in civil wars, many campesinos and farmers carried pistols, usually poked barrel-first into the tops of their pants. In recent years, this custom has become less common, but many will still carry or display some kind of weapon for protection, as land disputes continue to be a prevalent problem.

room schoolhouse as well. The homes are one- or two-room huts made from clay, adobe, or rough-hewn, unpainted boards, and they have palm-leaf roofs and bare dirt floors. In rural areas, few people can afford proper furniture for their basic homes. Electricity, refrigeration, and running water are very rare. Water must be carried by mule or cow from the nearest streams, sometimes miles away.

URBAN LIFE

Compared with campesinos, urban residents live in comfort, although there are few conveniences available by Western standards. Families still live together, and everyone who is old enough to work adds to the family income. Very few Hondurans can afford a car or the expensive imported gasoline it runs on. Most people travel by taxi or bus—both are affordable and comfortable.

The men who work in the cities of Tegucigalpa, San Pedro Sula, Puerto Cortés, and La Ceiba are often skilled workers who went to a trade school, and a few to a university. The head of the household, as well as any older sons, may be a mechanic, construction worker, furniture repairman, or an attendant at a filling station. With the influx of foreign investment during the past decade, many men also work in industries producing auto parts and machinery, safety and security equipment, building products, and electrical machinery. Some men may own a small business with their brothers or cousins. After work, they may stop to have a few drinks with other men before returning home.

The women who work in the cities are often teachers, secretaries, or domestic workers. During the past decade, larger numbers of women have

The Family Code passed in 1984 gave more rights to single mothers, requiring divorced men to help in the rearing of their children. However, despite these legal rights, in rural areas it is rare for mothers to receive any form of child support from children's fathers. Women do not have much agency in Honduras, so it is very difficult to bring up charges against men or fight back in any capacity.

moved into the manufacturing industries, working in clothing factories, food processing, and drinks industries. Women are responsible for cleaning, laundry, and cooking in their own homes, in addition to working outside the home all day. There are also more women attending college to become educated and improve their status.

DWELLINGS A family in the city can usually afford a small home with an open patio and a red-tiled roof. Many people live in one-room apartments. Some homes have a small kitchen as well. The family traditionally gathers around the kitchen table at the end of the day to discuss events and share stories.

A Honduran family poses together at their father's grocery store in Choluteca.

EDUCATION

The educational system in Honduras is one of the least developed in Central America. United Nations statistics show that barely thirty-two out of every one hundred students finish primary school without repeating grades. Public education is free and obligatory for every Honduran child from age six to fifteen, but not every child receives this benefit. Many students, especially in rural areas, go to school for grades one and two and then leave school to work and help earn a living for the family, usually by helping out on the farm. Nevertheless, this is a major improvement. Before the education reforms of 1957, there was no national education system, and education was the privilege of

Young Honduran children sit in their classroom.

those wealthy enough to send their children to private institutions. In practice, this is still relatively true because of the shortage of schools and teachers, the poor wages and training of teachers, and the high cost of materials needed for public schools. The wealthy send their children to private schools, where there are better-educated and better-paid teachers, as well as more money for school supplies.

The Honduran education system follows the European model, where schools are run through the Ministry of Public Education, but all schools are supported by the Catholic Church, and catechism is taught in class. Schools in the cities are commonly divided into boys' and girls' schools.

There is typically only one teacher, usually female, for grades one and two. In most public schools, the teacher may have as many as eighty students in her classroom. Grades three to six also have one teacher per classroom. There are fewer students in the higher grades, but they are still too many for one teacher to give significant time and attention to each individual.

HIGHER EDUCATION After completing grade six, a small number of students continue their education. Grades seven to nine are considered "college," or secondary school. Here, students have a different teacher for each subject.

Grades ten through twelve are called trade schools, or technical schools. Students who complete trade school may then become teachers, computer technicians, carpenters, and so on. Many women aspire to become teachers.

There are a few universities in Honduras, and less than 8 percent of children enrolled at primary level continue to university-level education. The National Autonomous University of Honduras (Universidad Nacional Autónoma de Honduras—UNAH) is the main school of higher learning. Located in Tegucigalpa, the UNAH was founded in 1847 and became an autonomous institution in 1957. The university also has branches in San Pedro Sula and La Ceiba. Hondurans go to college to become doctors, lawyers, professors, and engineers. More and more women go to college today. There are more Honduran students leaving Honduras to go to college as well.

Zamorano Pan-American Agricultural University, shown here, is located outside Tegucigalpa.

LITERACY RATES

In Honduras, approximately 89 percent of the population was considered to have reached a basic level of literacy by age fifteen, according to a 2015 estimate. Illiteracy rates vary depending on where Hondurans live. In rural settlements, especially in the western sections, more than 80 percent of the people cannot read and write. In the highlands near the capital and in the cities along the northern coast, illiteracy is much lower. The government is attempting to combat illiteracy, but because it is difficult to enforce the compulsory education law in remote areas, progress has been slow.

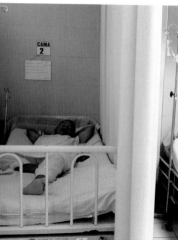

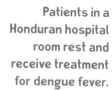

Patients in a Honduran hospital room rest and receive treatment for dengue fever.

HEALTH CARE

The quality of health care and access to it vary depending on location and income levels. In rural areas, access to trained medical personnel is limited. In isolated regions, there are almost no doctors. Rural inhabitants have to travel to Tegucigalpa or San Pedro Sula to receive quality medical care, but the cost of care and travel prevent many Hondurans from getting proper treatment.

The lack of medical care for the majority of Hondurans is apparent in their poor health. Poverty also imposes restrictions on the food they eat, so malnutrition is widespread, causing many young children to have stunted growth. According to the WHO, three-quarters of Hondurans lack proper vitamins for good health. A basic diet of corn, beans, and rice—which is the staple for most poor, rural Hondurans—does not cover all their dietary and health needs. In 2017, the infant mortality rate was estimated to be 17.2 deaths per 1,000 live births—an improvement over previous years, but still high. Average life expectancy in 2017 was estimated to be sixty-nine for men and seventy-three for women.

A significant share of the population lacks access to running water and sanitation facilities. Infectious and parasitic diseases are the leading causes of death. Diseases caused by poor sanitation and poor water quality include bacterial diarrhea, hepatitis A, and typhoid. Alcoholism and drug addiction are also common health problems. In the cities, there has been a dramatic rise in human immunodeficiency virus (HIV) infections that cause acquired immune deficiency syndrome (AIDS). As of 2016, an estimated twenty-one thousand people are living with AIDS in Honduras . The disease is spreading through intravenous drug use, prostitution, and rape.

Tropical diseases like dengue fever, malaria, and Chagas disease are also easily transmitted due to the high prevalence of insects, the humid environment, and water contamination. Insects are a common cause of disease in Honduras. About six hundred thousand Hondurans are affected by Chagas disease, which usually starts with a high fever and swelling of the eyelids on the side of the face near the bite wound. Later in life, the disease can reappear and attack vital organs such as the heart and colon. The disease is spread by chinches, blood-sucking bugs, which tend to attack their victims at night. Dengue is a mosquito-borne viral infection. The infection causes a flu-like illness and occasionally develops into a potentially lethal complication called severe dengue. The same mosquitos that carry dengue fever can also transmit chikungunya, yellow fever, and Zika infection.

Hurricane Mitch brought further health-related problems to the country in November 1998. Water contaminated by widespread death and destruction carried deadly diseases such as malaria and cholera. International relief brought in water purification machines and vaccinations against such diseases to help keep down the spread of fatal illnesses. Thousands suffered from respiratory illnesses, including pneumonia, after the rains.

Most Hondurans do not relate their health problems to their real causes, like malnutrition, sanitation, or environmental hazards. When a state of affairs has existed for generations—there has not been a dramatic food shortage, for example, but the diet has been continually inadequate—people fail to make the connection between poor diet and poor health. Their long-term poverty also means they have few options. Stunted children, infectious diseases, mental retardation, constant tiredness, and low productivity are viewed as normal because they have been the norm for centuries. Many Hondurans have never known what a healthy, nourished, comfortable life feels like.

INTERNET LINKS

https://www.international.gc.ca/cil-cai/country_insights-apercus_pays/ci-ic_hn.aspx?lang=eng
This page includes cultural tips for conversation when traveling to Honduras.

http://www.who.int/en
Visit this World Health Organization site to learn about the health and risks of going to Honduras.

RELIGION

A colonial-era church stands at the center of Copán Ruinas.

8

RELIGION AND TRADITION ARE extremely important to many Hondurans. Religion influences Hondurans daily through their dress and the holidays and festivals they celebrate. Historically, Roman Catholicism was the country's dominant religion. In recent years, however, the population has become more evenly split between Catholics and Protestants, including members of the rapidly growing Evangelical Protestant movement. Many Hondurans in the more remote areas of the country have mixed their primary Christian religion with ancient indigenous ceremonies, superstitions, and magic. Religion is extremely ingrained into the daily life of the Honduran population even though the constitution guarantees religious freedom and the separation of church and state.

The Black Carib people, or the Garifuna, still maintain their own religious system. It is a mixture of African and Amerindian traditions, but it includes Catholic elements. The Garifuna consider dreams and possession rituals important ways of accessing their spiritual consciousness. Their religious practice combines belief in saints with reverence toward gubida *(the spirits of ancestors) and faith in shamans or "spirit helpers" (called* buwiyes). *Their religious practices—including dancing, singing, drumming, and use of alcohol—have long been considered suspicious by outsiders. People unaccustomed to these religious practices have accused the Garifuna of paganism and devil worship.*

CATHOLIC SACRAMENTS Hondurans begin their introduction to the Catholic religion by being baptized. If a small town does not have its own priest, it is customary to wait for a fiesta (celebration) when a priest will come to celebrate the festival and, at that time, perform all the town's baptisms at once. A fiesta usually follows a baptism, and the whole extended family attends. Being baptized is extremely important in the Catholic faith.

After a Catholic marriage ceremony, where there is an exchange of rings and vows, a fiesta is held in the home of either the bride or groom's parents—usually at the house of whoever is wealthier. After food and drink at the house, the celebration shifts to a larger hall for a dance if the budget allows.

Catholic funerals are absolutely traditional within Catholic families. Immediately after death, the family holds a *novena*, or nine nights of prayer in front of the saint's altar at home. Novenas are also often held six months after the death and on its first anniversary. Close friends and family are invited to novenas.

PROTESTANTISM

Evangélicos (eh-van-HAY-lee-kohs) are Protestant groups that have emerged as important religious forces since the 1980s. Few Hondurans who profess to be Evangelicals belong to the mainstream Protestant denominations, such as Lutheranism. Today, the largest Evangelical churches in the country are

the Methodists, the Southern Baptists, the Central American Mission, the Abundant Life Church, and the charismatic Pentecostal denomination, the Assemblies of God.

The largest population of Protestants is made up of the English-speaking inhabitants of the Bay Islands. This geographical religious split is due to the fact that the British were the main influence in the Bay Islands, not the Roman Catholic Spanish who ruled the mainland.

Evangelical Christians pray together in the Evenezzer Church in San Pedro Sula, Honduras.

CHURCHES

Places of worship in Honduras include Catholic and Protestant churches that vary from extravagant, ornate basilicas presided over by a bishop to meager, thatched-roof buildings in small towns, with no priests at all. Paintings and states of saints decorate the Roman Catholic churches regardless of the town's wealth.

Catholics may go to church to pray to a saint different from the one they venerate in their own home. Masses are held on Sundays, mostly in Spanish, but there are services in English in the larger cities.

The Protestant Evangelical churches are newer and simpler in style, reflecting their belief that the church is made of people, not walls. English services are more common in Evangelical churches due to the British and American influence in the spread of the Protestant faith.

OTHER RELIGIONS

The immigrant population accounts for the presence of other religions in Tegucigalpa and San Pedro Sula. They include Judaism (Jews), Church of Jesus Christ of Latter-Day Saints (Mormons), and Mennonite Protestantism. There are also a few indigenous tribal religions, as well as some African religious traditions practiced by the Black Caribs on the north coast. The Church of Jesus Christ of Latter-Day Saints erected a temple in Tegucigalpa in February of 2013. The Tegucigalpa Honduras Temple is the first to be built in Honduras and the sixth in Central America.

TRADITIONAL BELIEFS

Some indigenous customs and traits have survived in the otherwise Catholic and Protestant communities. Although the power of folk beliefs has declined over the centuries, many Hondurans believe that certain people have the power to do good or evil based on magic and psychic or supernatural forces. In remote areas, people consult priests for advice on marriage, feuds with neighbors, and times of bad luck, much like their ancestors consulted the medicine man.

FOLK MEDICINE

Many Hondurans have very limited access to modern Western medicine, especially in rural areas. Therefore, folk medicine plays an important role, particularly for the poor and those who live in remote regions. Towns usually have a spiritual person who is known for handling illnesses, reminiscent of a traditional medicine man, who is called upon to prescribe herbs and say prayers. Sometimes this person is a midwife, and occasionally it is the storekeeper who sells traditional cures.

Massage and purging are common practices to rid a person of his or her sickness. Many Hondurans also believe foods belong to the "hot" or "cold" category and that one or the other should be avoided or prescribed to cure common ailments. "Hot" foods include coffee, oranges, and beef. "Cold" foods include coconuts, bananas, salt, and most kinds of seafood. Herbs are also divided into hot or cold and are used to treat illnesses.

A Mayan priest prays to praise the gods and ask for a plentiful harvest.

INTERNET LINKS

http://www.catholic-hierarchy.org/country/dhn2.html
This site provides information on the history of the Catholic Church in Honduras.

https://www.hondurastravel.com/news/culture/our-lady-of-suyapa
This tourist site offers information and photos of the Basilica of the Virgin of Suyapa.

LANGUAGE

A doctor talks to a group of Hondurans about the importance of medical checkups.

9

THE OFFICIAL LANGUAGE OF Honduras is Spanish, and it is the most widely spoken language in the region. English, however, is the main language of the Bay Islands. English is also spoken to some extent in the large cities, and it is spoken more frequently in Protestant religious services. A few indigenous languages are still spoken today in remote regions.

HONDURAN SPANISH

Just as the colonial Spanish explorers brought their customs, they also brought their language. However, like most Latin American countries, Hondurans do not speak Castilian Spanish, the official standard Spanish of Spain that originated in the Castile region.

Like most Romance languages, Spanish has masculine and feminine nouns and adjectives. Masculine nouns generally end in *o* and feminine nouns end in *a*, and the adjectives used to describe the nouns must agree with their gender. For example, "the little boy" is *el chiquito muchacho* (el chee-KEE-toh moo-CHAH-choh). "The little girl" is *la chiquita muchacha* (lah chee-KEE-tah moo-CHAH-chah).

HONDURAS'S UNWRITTEN LANGUAGES

Some indigenous languages in Honduras do not have a written alphabet or text. Pech of northeastern Honduras is an example. In an attempt to keep the Pech language alive in the midst of the predominantly Spanish Honduran culture, some linguists have been working in recent years to develop a written language. But first these linguists, together with Pech teachers, had to create an alphabet.

Pech has a very complicated vowel system—long vowels, short vowels, nasal vowels, glottal vowels, and vowels with an aspiration after them. But most complicated of all, Pech has high and low tones that are very difficult to represent in writing.

Many people have collaborated on this project, and the first two books in Pech were printed in 1996 using the new alphabet. A Spanish-Pech dictionary and books for second graders have also been published. The Pech have expressed their gratitude for the effort to preserve their language by naming one of their schools after a Honduran linguist who worked on the project.

Spanish also has formal and informal forms of words. The familiar form of "you" is *tú*, and the more formal form is *usted*. In daily conversations between Hondurans who know one another well, the familiar tú is used.

Hondurans, like other Latin Americans, often use diminutives to soften what they are saying, making speech more familiar, affectionate, and compassionate. For instance, instead of saying *momento* (moh-MAIN-toh), which means "a moment," they will say *momentito* (moh-main-TEE- toh), which makes "Just a minute!" sound a little more apologetic.

There are several indigenous languages spoken in Honduras, including Garifuna, Miskito, Sumo, Pech, and Jicaque. It is estimated that fewer than one thousand people speak the Pech language today.

OTHER LANGUAGES

English is the main language spoken in the Bay Islands. Black and white immigrants from the Antilles, the main group of islands in the West Indies, and from Belize (formerly called British Honduras) settled in the Bay Islands near the end of the colonial period and have kept their island version of English alive. Arabic is also spoken on the Bay Islands by immigrants from the Middle East.

Traditional Native languages are mostly isolated within remote indigenous communities. However, there are various slang words in the Spanish-speaking Ladino culture that are indigenous in origin. There are also many names of places, towns, and streets that are derived from Nahuatl, the language of the Mexican allies of the Spanish conquerors. The Pipil people near the El Salvadoran border still speak a language related to Nahuatl. The largest indigenous group, the Lencas, speak various dialects of their language, although Spanish is being adopted by their communities today.

A Honduran woman greets a friend with an affectionate kiss.

GESTURES

Hondurans use their hands and arms a great deal when they speak, especially when they are passionate about a subject. In general, they gesticulate more than Americans do.

In the city, when people greet one another, it is expected that women kiss women, men kiss women, and women kiss men. Hondurans will also gesture to others with their lips, especially if they are gossiping about that person.

EXPRESSIONS

Terms of endearment are most important in Honduras because the people are very friendly, warm, and caring. Adults speaking to children will often use the term *niño* (NEE-nyo) or *niña* (NEE-nya), which means "child." When Hondurans want to use a term of endearment for a beloved sister or female cousin or friend, they use the term *tita* (TEE-tah). When speaking to a brother or male cousin or friend, they use the term *tito* (TEE-toh). When children want to use a term of endearment for either their mother or grandmother, they say

Lengua de Señas Hondureñas (LESHO) is a sign language developed for the deaf in Honduras, much like American Sign Language (ASL). For every language and dialect there is a new sign language.

mamita (mah-MEE-tah). And when speaking to their father or grandfather, they say *papito* (pa-PIH-toh). Otherwise children refer to parents as "mom" and "pa," or *mamá* (mah-MAH) and *papá* (pah-PAH). But they are careful not to put the accent in the wrong place for papá, because "PAH-pah" means "potato" or "Pope"!

Chickens and roosters have come to play a large role in Honduran folktales and expressions. They use the term "henpecked" in an unusual context—from a joke about a Honduran president's parrot that was pecked free of its feathers by chickens in a henhouse. They also use the expression *Este es mi gallo* (EHS-teh ehs mee GAH-yo), which means "This is my rooster." This expression was originally used by Hondurans who would bet on a winning rooster during a cockfight, but today it is used to mean something along the lines of "This is mine and it is the best!"

POLITE COMMUNICATION

Business letters in Honduras often begin with an elaborate, fervent, positive greeting, even if the rest of the letter is terribly negative. For example, a common opening sentence would be: "I hope that this letter finds you in the

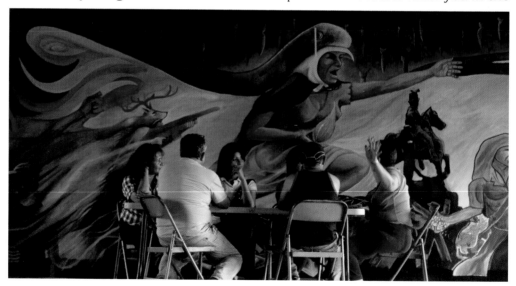

Hondurans gather under a mural that is critical of the coup that ousted former president Manuel Zelaya. Even when discussing politics, politeness is expected in Honduran culture.

best of health and that all of your family and loved ones are healthy and prospering." A short, brisk letter would appear rude and altogether unkind to a Honduran.

Hondurans are more verbal than many cultures. Instead of quietly slinking late into a meeting that has started, the latecomer must call out a greeting. Hondurans forgive lateness, but not a person who forgets to say *Buenos dias* (BWAY-nos DEE-as). They exchange this in greeting when they meet and say *Buenas noches* (BWAY-nas NAW-chez) when they part. To pass one another without a greeting would be considered very rude.

When sitting down with someone who is eating, whether he or she is a relative or a business acquaintance, well-mannered Hondurans sit down and say *Buen provecho* (boo-en pro-VEH-cho), which means "Much good may it do you!"

THE SPANISH ALPHABET

Spanish uses the Roman alphabet, like English. There are, however, a few differences. In Spanish, *ch*, *ll*, and *rr* are considered to be single, separate letters. When speaking, *rr* is rolled stronger and longer than a single *r*. The double *l* (*ll*), on the other hand, sounds more like a *y*. The letter *ñ* is also a separate letter. *B* and *v* have the same sound. *H* is not pronounced, and *j* is pronounced like *h*. *K* and *w* do not exist in the Spanish language, but these letters are found in foreign words that have been adopted by Hondurans.

NAMES

Popular first names in Honduras for girls are Suyapa (named after the Virgin of Suyapa), Ana, Janice, and Maria. Popular names for boys include Mario, Carlos, José, and Antonio.

Hondurans follow the Spanish custom of forming a double surname by taking the family surname of each parent. For instance, a young woman by the name of Teresa Vásquez González has two surnames—González from her mother and Vásquez from her father. Formally, she is known as Señorita Vásquez. If she marries a man by the name of Juan Carboñera García, she

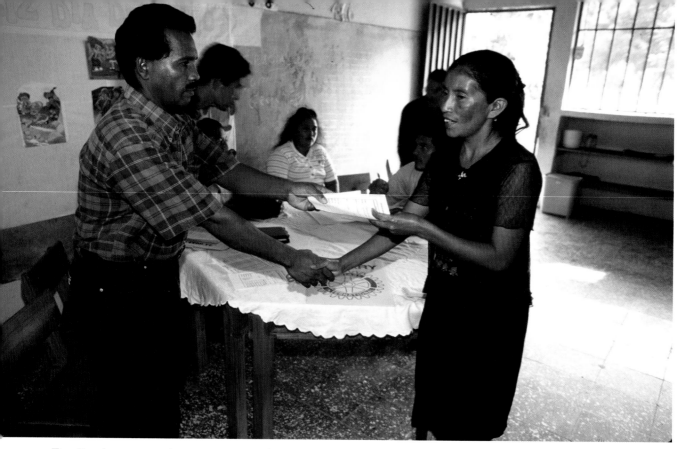

Two Hondurans meet, shake hands, and exchange pleasant conversation in Puente Alto, Honduras.

keeps her father's surname but replaces her mother's surname with that of her husband's father, often adding *de* in the middle. Thus, she would become Teresa Vásquez de Carboñera, or Señora de Carboñera.

For men, after the first mention of their full name, they are called by their father's surname—for instance, Oscar Calderón Hernández is referred to as Señor Oscar Calderón. However, some men prefer to use both surnames.

TITLES

Titles are also important in Honduras. Becoming a teacher, lawyer, professor, engineer, architect, or doctor takes a lot of work and determination. Therefore, Hondurans believe that a professional person has earned his or her title and should be spoken of with it. Just as Americans say Doctor Jones, Hondurans say Doctor Moreno, as well as Teacher Avila, Professor Martinez, and Attorney Nuñez.

PRINT MEDIA

As a poor country with a low rate of literacy, Honduras has few local newspapers compared to many countries. Popular local newspapers in Spanish include La Tribuna, Tiempo, El Heraldo, *and* La Prensa, *while English-language newspapers include* Honduras This Week. *The country of Honduras only recognizes the government-run newspaper,* La Gaceta, *for official notices. Many of the newspapers are linked to local political and business interests. The government regulates journalists closely, requiring that all reporters be registered in the College of Journalists and that all news editors be Honduran by birth. Journalists in Honduras tend to practice self-censorship when reporting on any topics about which the government or wealthy elite might be sensitive. Reporters have been prosecuted for publishing articles deemed anti-government in the past, and journalists have been vulnerable to violence by powerful nongovernment groups.*

Respect for elders is extremely important for Hondurans. A male adult is Señor and a female adult who is married is Señora. Someone who is a very well respected member of a community earns the higher title of Don for a man or Doña for a woman. If these terms were not used, a person would be very insulted. There is a difference between the big cities and the small villages. In cities, it is common to always use the terms Señor or Señora. In the villages, Don and Doña are the most acceptable titles when speaking with respect.

INTERNET LINKS

http://www.onlinenewspapers.com/honduras.htm
You can read the online editions of Honduran newspapers here.

https://www.youtube.com/watch?v=56OXP92SUBQ
This video can teach you the Spanish alphabet and correct pronunciation.

ARTS

Both dancing and folk music are important
parts of Honduran culture.

10

D ANCE, PAINTING, POETRY, AND folk crafts showcase traditional Honduran beliefs and folklore, as well as some new modern influences. The arts also encompass the rich blend of cultures within Honduran identity. Both Ladino traditions and indigenous traditions are celebrated in Honduran art. In recent years, promotion of the arts has been intensified through both public and private institutions. These institutions organize exhibitions, contests, and events where new and old generations of artists can come together and exhibit their work.

DANCE

Dancing is a vital part of Honduran culture. Each department has its own traditional dance. Boys and girls learn this and perform it at festivals. Almost every girl has a traditional dress, always bright and colorful, to be worn on these occasions. Women's skirts are full, and the blouses have ruffled collars and sleeves. Men wear full pants and ruffled shirts as well. Many official folk dance groups exist in the cities, whose members

"The poor are many
and so—
impossible to forget.
...
They
can steady the coffin
of a constellation on
    their shoulders.
They can wreck
the air like furious
    birds,
blocking out the sun.

But not knowing
    these gifts,
they enter and exit
    through mirrors of
    blood,
walking and dying
    slowly.

And so,
one cannot forget
    them.

—"The Poor" by
Roberto Sosa

The drums beat loudly as Hondurans gather around, and the dancers begin to clap and stomp their feet. Faces are illuminated by firelight. Wide smiles and bright eyes reflect enthusiasm. A young female dancer darts out into the middle of the circle formed by the crowd and begins to dance with swinging hips and small steps toward the drummers. A moment passes, then a young man joins her in the circle. He dances before her while the audience sends out cheers of encouragement. This is punta. *Punta is traditionally performed at wakes, but it is also a popular dance style.*

Juan Ramón Molina (1875-1908) was a national Honduran poet and a visionary. His collection *Tierras, Mares y Cielos* (Lands, seas and skies), is a national favorite. The National Library of Honduras was named after him in 2009, and in 1954, a bridge was named after him.

are older students. Competitions are intense and attract a large audience. Groups from universities are considered professional. Young girls look up to these university dancers and aspire to be as talented when they are older.

There are hundreds of well-known traditional dances in Honduras. The *maladio wanaragua* (mah-LAH-dee-oh wah-nah-RAH-gwah) is a mask dance that represents the fight of the Garifuna against England. The *sique* (seek) dance has its origins in the dances of the early indigenous people. Another popular dance on the north coast is the *mascaro* (mas-KAH-roh), which shows strong African influences. Hondurans also love common Latin American dances such as the samba and salsa.

The Garifuna (Black Caribs) of the northern coast have a very important dance that originated on the island of Saint Vincent in the Caribbean. The *punta* (POOHN-tah) is traditionally danced when a relative dies so that the spirit stays on Earth. It is also said to be a dance invoking fertility. However, the influence of the punta has stretched far beyond traditional boundaries. Young girls learn the dance from older sisters. Teenagers and young adults do the punta in discos around the country. And people come from all around the world to watch the original punta dancers, the Garifuna, in the city of La Ceiba.

MUSIC

It is common to hear the music of a marimba band in full swing at any hour of the day or night. Like all Latin Americans, Hondurans love music. They love boleros or anything with a cha-cha rhythm and a lively beat. Honduran music has developed into varied rhythms and styles recalling the religious and folkloric traits of each ethnic group. There are few professional musical groups aside from marimba bands.

There are a few classical music groups and a symphony orchestra, too. Two large annual music festivals bring both symphony and folk composers and performers together to celebrate music. Based in La Ceiba, Guillermo Anderson was Honduras's best-known musician, combining punta, rock, and salsa for a very Honduran sound. Some consider his song "En Mi Pais" (In My Country) an alternative national anthem in Honduras. Anderson passed away in 2016.

The guitar is a popular musical instrument in Honduras.

The marimba is the best-loved and most representative instrument of Central America. It was introduced to Honduras by African slaves, but its origin can be traced from Southeast Asia, through Africa, to Latin America. Modern adaptations and improvements of the instrument are attributed to Central America. A *marimbero* (mah-rim-BAY-roh) is a person who plays the marimba. There are various forms of the marimba, but usually a whole ensemble, not just one person, plays a large, multifaceted one. Members of a marimba ensemble are usually men from the same family. There are a few women ensembles today, but a mixed gender group would be quite unusual. Boys and girls play in separate groups at school.

Other popular musical instruments are the *caramba* (cah-RAHM-bah), a string instrument found mostly in rural areas, and the guitar.

OTHER PERFORMING ARTS

Honduras does not have a major theater tradition. There are small drama groups, and towns and villages have their own small groups that dramatize religious stories during festivals.

Traditional puppet shows are performed in some towns and cities and are enjoyed by both children and adults.

The Basilica of Our Lady of Suyapa, near Tegucigalpa, is one of Honduras's most iconic structures.

ARCHITECTURE

The ornate temples and elaborately constructed buildings and pyramids of the ancient Maya influence how modern Hondurans build and decorate their buildings. Tegucigalpa's Concordia Park is dedicated to the memory of the Maya. It features a miniature Mayan temple that shows their distinctive and elaborate ornamentation. In the larger cities of Honduras, intricate carvings and designs of the pre-Columbian era have been artfully integrated into Spanish colonial architecture.

A central plaza, or square, forms the heart of most towns. Important government buildings face it, as does a Catholic chapel or cathedral. The colonial influence—large, arched doorways and domes atop churches—is seen in many buildings in the plazas. These old-style buildings stand in stark contrast to the skyscrapers in Tegucigalpa and San Pedro Sula, which use the latest building materials, technology, and design. They house mostly government offices and

Velásquez is probably the most celebrated Honduran painter. He is internationally known for his primitivist paintings of his village of San Antonio de Oriente, a sixteenth-century mining center high in the mountains southeast of Tegucigalpa. Velásquez was a barber by profession, without any formal artistic training. He began to paint in 1927 and moved to San Antonio de Oriente in 1930, where he was the town barber and telegraph operator. His unique primitive paintings reflect the humble tranquility of that village where he spent most of the next thirty years of his life.

Velásquez and his paintings were not discovered until 1943, when he met Dr. Wilson Popenoe, director of the Zamorano Agricultural University. Popenoe hired him as a barber at the school but encouraged him to market his paintings in Tegucigalpa, where they sold for low prices. In 1954, Popenoe organized an exhibition of Velásquez's paintings in Washington, DC, where the artist gained international acclaim. In 1955, he was given the National Prize for Art, Honduras's most important award for art. He was also elected mayor of San Antonio de Oriente. Velásquez's son and grandson have carried on his primitivist traditions. Velásquez's work is on permanent display in many of Tegucigalpa's finest hotels and galleries.

big, often foreign, businesses. In front of these modern buildings there are still the quaint, shaded cantinas where many Hondurans feel most comfortable.

VISUAL ARTS

Painting makes up the strongest base in the modern artistic development of Honduras. Most people believe that the fine arts in Honduras were founded by José Miguel Gómez in the eighteenth century with his religious paintings. Although they show a European influence, they have a distinctly Honduran style. Contemporary Honduran painting began in the 1920s. Today, self-taught painters all over the country are dedicated to depicting beautiful, primitive Honduran landscapes and modest towns.

One of the best-known painters in Honduras is Arturo López Rodezno (1908—1975). To train new artists, he founded the National School of Arts and Crafts. His paintings and school have influenced artists in Honduras and all over the world. José Antonio Velásquez is famous for his paintings depicting life in his village, San Antonio de Oriente, which give the world a window into Honduran life. His most famous painting is of Tegucigalpa's main square with the statue of Francisco Morazán.

A favorite painter in Honduras is Luis Padilla, who is known for his use of vibrant colors, especially red. His work is considered enigmatic, suggestive, impressionistic, and contemporary. He claims inspiration from Van Gogh and a contemporary Guatemalan artist, Elmar Rojas. Cruz Bermudez is a Garifuna painter who loves natural settings and paints endangered species to publicize environmental issues.

A popular theme in painting is the "rain of fish," showing hundreds of fish raining down from the sky. It is based on a Honduran phenomenon where villagers in the department of Yoro woke up after a June thunderstorm to find the ground strewn with fish! One explanation of the strange event is that these fish followed a low-pressure system in from the sea near the end of their lifespan. They leapt ashore during the storm and suffocated. It is not hard to imagine why this fantastic event has inspired so many painters over the years.

LITERATURE

Authors in Honduras traditionally started their careers as newspaper journalists because there were not many local magazines. Honduran newspapers typically print poems, essays, and short stories, so budding writers can publish and polish their work in the papers and at the same time develop a readership. An author who has a following would then approach a publisher with a novel or a collection of poems, essays, or short stories and may pay to have the work published. Because of the cost involved in becoming a published writer, authors in Honduras are often wealthy and not representative of the common Honduran.

José Trinidad Reyes (1797–1855)

Reyes, known as the Father of Higher Education in Honduras, was multitalented—a playwright, poet, politician, and educator. He was born in Tegucigalpa to poor parents, and his humble origins prevented him from furthering his studies in Comayagua. He went to Nicaragua, where he graduated with a degree in philosophy, theology, and canon law. In 1822, he was ordained a Catholic priest. In 1840, he was named bishop of Honduras by Rome, but political intrigue prevented him from assuming this position. Reyes was opposed to the president of Honduras, Francisco Zelaya y Ayes, so the president told Rome that Reyes had died! Under a new president, Reyes turned a literary academy into Honduras's main university, the Universidad Nacional Autónoma de Honduras. He was named its first rector. In 1846, Reyes was named poet laureate of Honduras. He is known for bringing the first piano to Tegucigalpa. Reyes's book on physics was a textbook in Honduras for many years.

Lucila Gamero de Medina (1873–1964)

Medina wrote the first Honduran novel to be published. She was an amazing woman for her time—a physician, an essayist, a feminist, and a novelist. She published many novels during her long and productive life. Her first two novels, Amalia Montiel *and* Adriana y Margarita, *were published in Tegucigalpa in 1893 when she was only twenty years old. They are still read today. Her most famous novel is* Blanca Olmedo *(1903), a controversial attack on the Catholic clergy. Medina was an intelligent, talented, and ambitious woman whom Honduran women admire and try to emulate.*

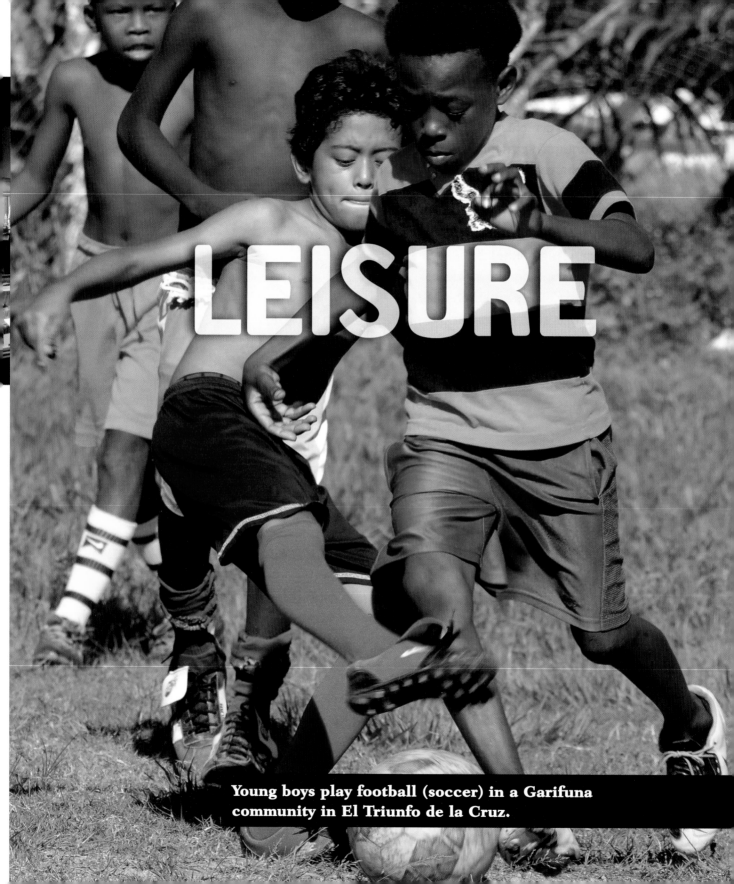

LEISURE

Young boys play football (soccer) in a Garifuna community in El Triunfo de la Cruz.

M ANY HONDURANS DO NOT HAVE A lot of time or money for leisure activities due to crippling poverty and labor-intensive jobs. The leisure activities in which they do participate, such as football (soccer), dancing, and singing, are highly valued. Most Hondurans spend their leisure time with their families, as family life holds a special place in Honduran culture. And it is not uncommon for families to spend much of their leisure time together watching—or even playing—football.

FOOTBALL

Football, or as Americans call it, soccer, is by far the most popular sport for boys and men to play, as well as to watch. Association football, as soccer is called in Honduras, is the national sport, and it is run by the Federación Nacional Autónoma de Fútbol de Honduras (FENAFUTH). In order to become a hero, one need only be an outstanding soccer player. Honduran boys can enjoy a fast game of soccer, while claiming it is too hot to work in the fields. Hondurans passionately follow the sport at the local, national, and international levels. Emotions often run high. Hondurans listen to big games on the radio, as many people do not have television. Almost every town has a soccer team.

11

The national football team of Honduras has three World Cup appearances to its name, having made its debut in Spain in 1982, where the team recorded two ties in its best performance to date.

Due to how expensive making a movie is, the film industry of Honduras is relatively small. Even so, there have been quite a few films to come out of Honduras. Some of the notable films have been Mas Allá de una Esperanza *(Beyond Hope), a documentary film by Francisco Andino;* Anita, La Cazadora de Insectos *(Anita, the Insect Hunter), directed by Hispano Durón;* Almas de la Media Noche *(Souls of Midnight), directed by Juan Carlos Fanconi;* Amor y Frijoles *(Love and Beans), by Mathew Kodath and Hernan Pereira; and* Unos Pocos con Valor *(A Few with Courage), directed by Douglas Martin.*

Movie theaters are located mostly in the urban centers and near tourist areas. The films shown are generally imported American or other Western films. Many of the theaters have a discount night that attracts many of the locals.

OTHER SPORTS

Basketball is quickly becoming popular in the cities of Honduras. Private schools have teams for basketball, volleyball, tennis, and baseball. Golf is played near the bigger cities by wealthy men. Sports for women have not been very popular in Honduras, but a women's football initiative has been making strides in tackling gender inequality. There is also a women's national football team.

Sport fishing is also popular among the wealthy. Along the Caribbean coast and on the Bay Islands, people come from all over to fish for tuna, barracuda, shark, blue and white marlin, sailfish, wahoo, mahi-mahi, grouper, kingfish, and red snapper.

People also come from all over the world to dive and snorkel at the coral reefs of the Bay Islands. The water is warm and clear, and underwater visibility is very good. It is mostly the wealthier Hondurans who take part in these activities.

LEISURE TIME

Dance and song have long been very important to Hondurans. Young girls usually learn the traditional dance of their department, as well as the popular punta dance, at a young age. Many city girls go on to take ballet or other forms of dance classes. In the absence of sports activities for the majority of girls, dancing gives girls the physical activity and "team" fun they need.

People also enjoy going to the beach, especially during national holidays. Hondurans swim, sunbathe, picnic, and surf whenever they can. Other activities that may challenge the mind and pass away the hours include cards, chess, and checkers. But most often in the evenings, Hondurans simply spend time with their families discussing the day's events.

As in most large cities of the world, people who have the time, interest, and a little extra money take classes in almost anything. Tegucigalpa offers classes in acting, guitar, drawing, painting, chess, and many forms of dance.

FOLKTALES AND STORYTELLING

Storytelling is a popular activity among Honduran families, with grandparents and other elders passing their evenings telling children folktales. Dramatic storytelling is an event during festivals that the celebrants thoroughly enjoy. Some stories are intended to teach moral lessons. Others are told in the form of jokes.

One of the most popular characters in Honduran oral literature is the *duende*, a short man who lives in the woods. Some of the stories about duende are told by parents to frighten children so that they will not stray into the woods. The most famous theme for duende stories is his attempt to get young girls to fall in love with him.

A young Honduran girl sings, wearing a traditional dress.

INTERNET LINKS

http://americanfolklore.net/folklore/2010/07/central_american_folklore.html
This site offers information on Central American folklore.

http://www.fifa.com/worldcup/teams/team=43909/profile-detail.html
This is the website of the national Honduran football team.

FESTIVALS

A group of children and adults celebrate
a birthday in a Honduran village.

THERE ARE MANY NATIONAL holidays in Honduras. Both religious and secular holidays are recognized as national holidays. Due to the poverty and strife that pervades life for the majority of Hondurans, holidays are special and are celebrated with family and loved ones. Holidays are so important that employers are required to pay their employees for the days off. In 2017, sixteen days were listed as public holidays, when businesses would be closed. Most festivals are celebrated as street fairs with singing and traditional dancing. Extended families get together to spend the fiesta with each other.

SECULAR FESTIVALS

Many of the secular festival days are celebrated in a small way in the community. There are many days that honor people or ideas. Language Day is celebrated mostly in school by students participating in competitions.

Every year on April 12, Hondurans celebrate the Punta Gorda Festival. This is a uniquely Honduran festival, as it celebrates the arrival of the first Garifuna people on the island of Roatán.

FOOD

Lobster, red snapper fish, shrimp, rice and beans, and plantains make up this Honduran plate.

THE HONDURAN DIET CONSISTS OF staples that the majority of Hondurans can produce themselves. There is not a lot of variety when it comes to day-to-day meals for most people. Wealthy Hondurans, however, can afford to buy different varieties of food. Urban people are generally better nourished—because they buy what they need, their diet tends to have a better balance of food groups. However, most Hondurans in the cities do not eat well by American standards. Geography also plays a major factor in what people can eat. For example, Hondurans living near the coast eat more seafood. While the daily assortment of food does not change much, the role of food is still extremely important to Hondurans, so much so that feasts are a central part of every fiesta.

• • • • • • • • • • • •

Honduran food is tasty and sometimes spicy hot. Hondurans use chili peppers in their cooking to add heat. To add a depth of flavor to meals, tomatoes, soy sauce, salt, black pepper, cilantro, cumin, onions, sweet peppers, garlic, and beef or chicken stock cubes are used, especially as a soup base.

A popular snack and traditional side, plantains are a staple in Honduran cuisine.

FOOD STAPLES

The typical diet of a Honduran is based on corn. It is the most widely planted crop, cheapest in the marketplace, and grown all year-round. Women turn corn into tortillas every day. Corn tortillas are a component of almost every meal, whether as a vehicle for other foods, or to be eaten alone. Red beans are the main source of protein. Mixing beans together with corn provides a complete protein. When beans are eaten alone, the body misses out on the essential amino acids that mixing corn with beans provides. People in Honduras and other Central American countries have come to understand this, which is why beans and corn tortillas are eaten daily, sometimes at every meal.

White rice is also a staple food. Cassava, another important food, is a tropical plant with a large, starchy root. Plantains, which resemble bananas, are used in many recipes as well.

OTHER COMMON FOODS

Most rural families own a cow, and from the milk, the women make *cuajada* (kwah-HAH-dah), a kind of cottage cheese that is slightly different from the North American cottage cheese. Most Hondurans do not drink milk as a beverage but eat the cream, sour cream, and cheese the milk provides. Although almost every rural household raises chickens and pigs, it is a rare treat to have meat. On rare occasions, pork is eaten, perhaps as a dish at a feast during a fiesta. Fish is more commonly eaten, especially in coastal towns. Hondurans usually eat their fish fried or in soups and stews.

Fried bananas, a popular snack, are often sold in the marketplace. *Tajaditas* (tah-jah-DEE-tahs), or crispy fried banana chips, and sliced green mangoes sprinkled with salt and cumin are sold in bags on the street. Another popular food item is the tamale. These are made by filling a cornmeal casing with a variety of meats and vegetables, then wrapping it in a banana leaf and cooking it in boiling water. These are traditionally made around Christmastime, but they are now enjoyed year-round.

Green vegetables are often missing from the diet, but peppers, especially hot chili peppers, are eaten with many meals. Hondurans, especially the rural poor, also eat sweet bread. Among the people living on the Caribbean coast, coconut bread is eaten almost daily.

POPULAR DISHES

Nacatamales (nah-kah-tah-MAH-les)—large corn cakes stuffed with vegetables and meat—are usually bought in the marketplace or made by those who can afford meat. *Tapado* (tah-PAH-doh), a dish from the Black Caribs, is a stew made with meat or fish, vegetables, and cassava. *Sopa de mondongo* (SOH-pah de moan-DOAN-goh) is a stew made with chopped tripe, part of a cow's stomach.

Baleada (bah-lay-AH-dah) is another daily favorite. This is a warm corn or flour tortilla folded over refried beans, crumbled cheese, and sour cream. Baleadas are often sold cheaply at markets, street stands, or food shacks. Another favorite street food is *tortillas con quesillo*—two crisp, fried corn tortillas with melted white cheese between them. Fried chicken is also a favorite food.

Baleadas are a common Honduran street food.

When dining out, most Hondurans will order a national dish called the *plato típico* (typical dish) because it is filling and inexpensive, besides being a favorite. It includes a combination of beans, rice, tortillas, fried bananas, beef or fish, potatoes or cassava, cream, cheese, and a cabbage or tomato salad. Many restaurants in cities or small towns offer a cheap, large, fast meal to workers at lunchtime called *plato del día*. The meals differ from place to place but always include tortillas.

MANGOS

Mangos are a staple fruit in Honduras and are extremely versatile in their use. They are especially abundant in the Bay Islands. As they are a sweet and fleshy fruit, they can be eaten as both a sweet snack or as a compliment to a meaty, savory dish. Mangos are full of vitamins and antioxidants as well, so they can add a healthy kick to any dish. Some of the more contemporary ways to add mango to meals include adding it to a grilled cheese or quesadilla. Mango also compliments both pork and seafood.

BEVERAGES

Honduran adults drink coffee with almost every meal, but they do not often drink tea. As coffee is native to the region, this makes sense. *Culey* (KOO-lee) is a very sweet fruit juice drunk especially by children. *Guifiti* (gwee-FEE-tee) is a tea-like herbal drink that tickles the taste buds and is drunk to detoxify the body. Sodas and colas are found everywhere today, including a few local flavors like banana. Most Hondurans do not drink unflavored milk, but *licuados*, milk blended with fruit, are popular.

It is unusual for Hondurans to drink alcohol with a meal. Alcoholic drinks include *aguardiente* (ah-gwar-dee-EHN-teh), translated as "fire water," a homemade liquor that tastes of licorice, and wine, including *vino de coyol* (VEE-noh de KO-yohl), a sparkling wine made from the sap of the coyol palm. There are also four kinds of beer made and consumed in Honduras.

THE KITCHEN

Women almost always do the cooking. It is very rare to find a man cooking in the kitchen. In rural homes, kitchens are usually outdoors. A woman has an adobe and sand oven called a *lorena* (loh-REH-nah) for baking breads. These ovens have no door and are approximately waist-high. Women burn firewood in them for two hours to get the oven hot enough to bake bread. The dough sits in small pans that are placed into the oven by hand. After twenty minutes,

the bread is usually done, and the loaves are removed from the oven with a long wooden paddle.

A rural woman will often have a wood-fire stove going as well to fry food or boil stews. People who can afford it will have this stove indoors in a kitchen. But even in the cities, an indoor kitchen is not used by everyone.

A young Honduran girl cooks tortillas over a wood fire in El Naranjal, Honduras.

MEALS

Every meal is generally eaten at home. Children who have many miles to walk to school will eat a meal provided by the school during the day. Some people in the cities go to restaurants for supper on special occasions.

This typical Honduran breakfast consists of fried eggs, plantains, beans, and avocados. Corn tortillas accompany most meals.

Meals are seldom eaten around a table. If there is no table, the family sits on chairs around the room. Some families eat outdoors because the space inside is too small. Those who have a television may sit around and watch it while they eat. Otherwise, they eat and talk about their day. Wealthier people have a separate room for dining.

Meals are eaten with spoons, forks, and knives, and tortillas and breads are eaten held in the hand.

BREAKFAST The morning meal is eaten only after some of the morning chores are done. Breakfast may include a combination of the following: red beans and tortillas, eggs, cheese (often cuajada), plantains, salty butter on bread, coffee, and even homemade cereal with milk. Poor Hondurans have coffee with bread for breakfast.

LUNCH Lunch is usually more substantial than breakfast and may include meat if the family can afford it. A typical lunch would have white rice with pork, beef, or chicken, a soup made of red beans, fish or chicken, and tortillas. Culey is often drunk during lunch.

SUPPER Supper is generally a lighter meal than lunch. It usually includes a soup, red beans, eggs, plantains, butter, and tortillas. Meat is not commonly eaten at this meal, even by those who can afford it. Fried beans with onions eaten with a tortilla is popular.

DESSERT

Most Hondurans do not eat dessert because they cannot afford the luxury. Where there is dessert, perhaps at a fiesta, sweet cake and ice cream are favorites. *Dulce de rapadura* (DOOL-say de rah-pah-DUHR-ah), a candy made from sugarcane juice, is the most common Honduran dessert.

DULCE DE RAPADURA

A common candy in Honduras is dulce de rapadura, basically a processed sugar cube made from sugarcane and wrapped in cane leaves or cornhusks. Dulce, as it is called, is usually made by only one campesino in a given village. Sugarcane stalks are cut down and put through a sugar mill powered by cows attached to horizontal wooden braces. The cows walk in a circle to turn the press, and juice from the sugarcane is squeezed out.

The juice is collected, cooked, and then cooled in wooden molds. There may be as many as fifty large molds in one very large rectangular piece of wood. The end product is sold to other people in the village or taken to a market elsewhere. Aside from being eaten as candy, dulce is used to sweeten coffee, make fruit preserves, or sweeten breads.

INTERNET LINKS

https://www.frommers.com/destinations/honduras/food-drink
This travel guide explores the cuisine of Honduras.

http://www.traveltourxp.com/9-traditional-foods-to-relish -in-honduras
This article suggests food to try and love in Honduras.

MACHETEADAS (HONDURAN FRIED DOUGH)

These dense and sweet discs of fried dough are popular snacks in Honduras.

3 ⅓ cups (400 grams) all-purpose flour
1 teaspoon salt
1 teaspoon baking powder
¼ cup (60 milliliters) coconut oil
1¼ cups (300 mL) warm water
Canola oil for frying
Honey to drizzle

In a large bowl, combine flour, baking powder, coconut oil and salt.

Make a well in the center of the mixture and pour the water into it.

Work mixture gently until it forms a cohesive dough.

Transfer to a clean and lightly floured kneading area and work the dough gently for about five to seven minutes. The dough should feel soft and flexible.

Divide the dough into twelve equal pieces.

Grease your hands with a little oil and form the dough into twelve balls. Place the dough back into the bowl, cover with cloth, and let it rest for forty-five minutes.

Heat canola oil over medium-high heat.

Flour your working surface, and place the dough on it.

Flatten each ball with a rolling pin, and roll out until they are about 6 inches in diameter.

Make three to four slits in each macheteada. Fry each one until golden brown on both sides.

Drizzle with honey and serve!

ATOL DE ELOTE AL ESTILO HONDUREÑO (HONDURAN-STYLE CORN BEVERAGE)

2½ cups (438 g) white corn kernels uncooked (about 4 or 5 ears)
4 cups (960 mL) low-fat milk
2 sticks cinnamon
½ teaspoon cloves
½ teaspoon salt
4—5 tablespoons sugar

Blend corn kernels with 1 cup (240 mL) of milk on high until well incorporated and smooth.

Pass the mixture through a colander and set aside.

In a heavy-bottom pot, combine corn mixture, remaining milk, sugar, salt, cinnamon and cloves.

Cook over medium heat for about fifteen minutes, stirring constantly so it doesn't burn. The mixture will thicken as it cooks.

Remove from heat and serve hot.

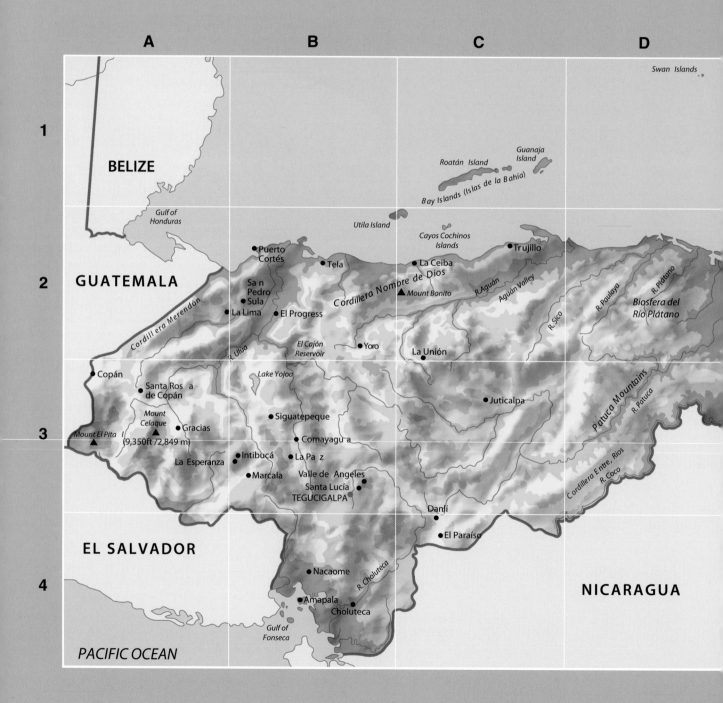

A　　**B**　　**C**　　**D**

1

2

3

4

BELIZE

Gulf of
Honduras

GUATEMALA

Swan Islands

Roatán Island

Guanaja
Island

Bay Islands (Islas de la Bahía)

Utila Island

Cayos Cochinos
Islands

Puerto
Cortés

Tela

La Ceiba
Dios

Trujillo

San
Pedro

Sula

La Lima

El Progress

Cordillera Nombre de Dios

▲ Mount Bonito

R.Aguán

Aguán Valley

R.Sico

R.Paulaya

R.Plátano

Biosfera del
Río Plátano

Cordillera Merendón

R. Ulúa

El Cajón
Reservoir

Yoro

La Unión

Copán

Lake Yojoa

Santa Rosa
de Copán

Juticalpa

Patuca Mountains

R.Patuca

Mount
Celaque

Mount El Pita l
(9,350ft /2,849 m)

Gracias

Siguatepeque

Comayagua

Intibucá

La Paz

La Esperanza

Marcala

Valle de Angeles

Santa Lucía

TEGUCIGALPA

Cordillera Entre Ríos

R.Coco

Danlí

El Paraíso

EL SALVADOR

NICARAGUA

Nacaome

R.Choluteca

Amapala

Choluteca

Gulf of
Fonseca

PACIFIC OCEAN

MAP OF HONDURAS

Caribbean Sea

Cajones Cays

Mosquito Coast

Caratasca Lagoon

● Puerto Lempira

● Capital city
● Major town
▲ Mountain peak

Feet	Meters
16,500	5,000
9,900	3,000
6,600	2,000
3,300	1,000
1,650	500
660	200
0	0

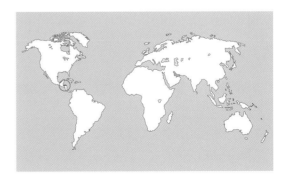

ECONOMIC HONDURAS

Services

 Airport

 Port

 Tourism

Natural Resources

 Hydroelectricity

 Lead

 Lumber

Palm oil

Petroleum

Silver

Agriculture

 Bananas

 Coffee

 Cotton

 Livestock

 Tobacco

Manufacturing

 Beverage

 Cement

 Chemical products

 Food processing

 Footwear & clothing

 Textiles

ABOUT THE ECONOMY

OVERVIEW

Honduras is the second-poorest country in Central America. The gap between the rich and the poor is very great, and unemployment has remained high for decades. The economy is dependent on just a few exports, especially bananas and coffee, making it vulnerable to natural disasters and changes in world prices. The United States is Honduras's largest trading partner, and the country relies heavily on the US economy. From 2010 to 2017, the economy grew 3.1—4.0 percent, which is a step in the right direction, though insignificant for the general population. In 2017, Honduras faced rising public debt, but its economy has performed better than expected due to low oil prices and improved investor confidence.

GROSS DOMESTIC PRODUCT (GDP)

$45.68 billion (2017 estimate)

GDP PER CAPITA

$5,500 (2017 estimate)

CURRENCY

Honduran lempiras (HNL)
$1 = 23.67 HNL (2018 estimate)

LABOR FORCE

3.735 million (2017 estimate)

LABOR FORCE BY TYPE OF JOB

Agriculture: 39.2 percent
Industry: 20.9 percent
Services: 39.8 percent (2005 estimate)

UNEMPLOYMENT RATE

5.9 percent (2017 estimate)

AGRICULTURAL PRODUCTS

Bananas, coffee, citrus, beef, timber, shrimp, tilapia, lobster, corn, African palm

NATURAL RESOURCES

Timber, gold, silver, copper, lead, zinc, iron ore, antimony, coal, fish, hydropower

MAIN INDUSTRIES

Sugar, coffee, textiles, clothing, wood products

MAIN EXPORTS

Coffee, apparel, shrimp, automobile wire harnesses, cigars, bananas, gold, palm oil, fruit, lobster, lumber, to US (36.7 percent), Germany (10.7 percent), El Salvador (8.6 percent) , Guatemala (6.5 percent), Netherlands (5.4 percent), Nicaragua (5.3 percent) (2016 estimate)

MAIN IMPORTS

Communications equipment, machinery and transport, industrial raw materials, chemical products, fuels, foodstuffs, from US (32.8 percent), China (14.1 percent), Guatemala (8.9 percent), Mexico (7.3 percent), El Salvador (5.7 percent) (2016 estimate)

CULTURAL HONDURAS

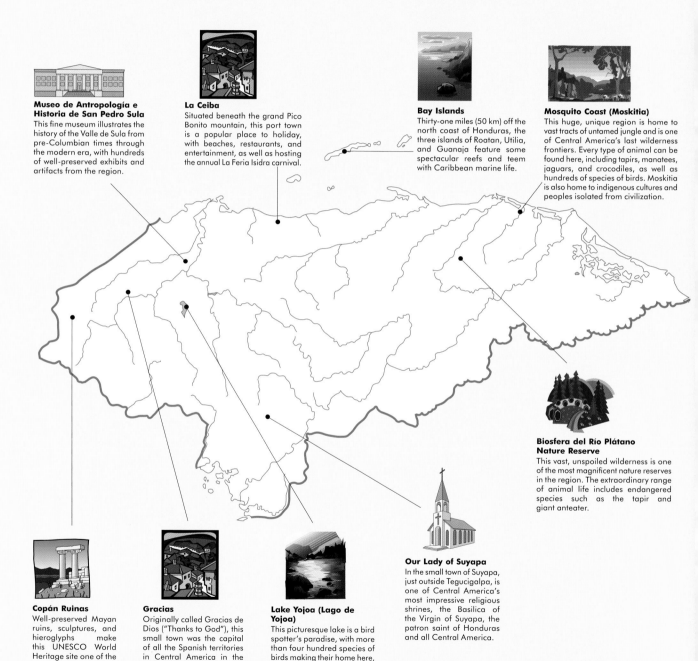

Museo de Antropología e Historia de San Pedro Sula
This fine museum illustrates the history of the Valle de Sula from pre-Columbian times through the modern era, with hundreds of well-preserved exhibits and artifacts from the region.

La Ceiba
Situated beneath the grand Pico Bonito mountain, this port town is a popular place to holiday, with beaches, restaurants, and entertainment, as well as hosting the annual La Feria Isidra carnival.

Bay Islands
Thirty-one miles (50 km) off the north coast of Honduras, the three islands of Roatan, Utilia, and Guanaja feature some spectacular reefs and teem with Caribbean marine life.

Mosquito Coast (Moskitia)
This huge, unique region is home to vast tracts of untamed jungle and is one of Central America's last wilderness frontiers. Every type of animal can be found here, including tapirs, manatees, jaguars, and crocodiles, as well as hundreds of species of birds. Moskitia is also home to indigenous cultures and peoples isolated from civilization.

Biosfera del Río Plátano Nature Reserve
This vast, unspoiled wilderness is one of the most magnificent nature reserves in the region. The extraordinary range of animal life includes endangered species such as the tapir and giant anteater.

Copán Ruinas
Well-preserved Mayan ruins, sculptures, and hieroglyphs make this UNESCO World Heritage site one of the great archaeological sites of Central America.

Gracias
Originally called Gracias de Dios ("Thanks to God"), this small town was the capital of all the Spanish territories in Central America in the sixteenth century. Today, it is home to many colonial-era buildings and cobbled streets.

Lake Yojoa (Lago de Yojoa)
This picturesque lake is a bird spotter's paradise, with more than four hundred species of birds making their home here, including the rare quetzal.

Our Lady of Suyapa
In the small town of Suyapa, just outside Tegucigalpa, is one of Central America's most impressive religious shrines, the Basilica of the Virgin of Suyapa, the patron saint of Honduras and all Central America.

ABOUT THE CULTURE

OFFICIAL NAME
Republic of Honduras

TOTAL AREA
43,278 square miles (112,090 sq km)

CAPITAL
Tegucigalpa

ADMINISTRATIVE DEPARTMENTS
18 departments (*departamentos*):
Atlántida, Choluteca, Colón, Comayagua,
Copán, Cortes, El Paraíso, Francisco
Morazán, Gracias a Dios, Intibucá, Islas
de la Bahía, La Paz, Lempira, Ocotepeque,
Olancho, Santa Bárbara, Valle, Yoro

HIGHEST POINT
Cerro Las Minas (Pico Celaque): 9,416 feet
(2,870 m) above sea level

POPULATION
9,038,741 (2017 estimate)

GENDER RATIO
1.01 male/female (2017 estimate)

AGE STRUCTURE:
0—14 years: 32.95%
15—24 years: 21%
25—54 years: 36.63%
55—64 years: 5.13%
65 years and over: 4.29% (2017 est.)

LIFE EXPECTANCY
Total population: 71.2 years
Male: 69.5 years
Female: 72.9 years (2017 estimate)

MEDIAN AGE
23 years (2017 estimate)

BIRTHRATE
22.4 births per 1,000 population
(2017 estimate)

DEATH RATE
5.3 deaths per 1,000 population
(2017 estimate)

ETHNIC GROUPS
Mestizo (mixed Amerindian and European)
90 percent, Amerindian 7 percent, black 2
percent, white 1 percent

RELIGION
Roman Catholic 46 percent, Protestant 41
percent, atheist 1 percent, other 2 percent,
none 9 percent (2014 estimate)

LANGUAGES
Spanish, Amerindian dialects

NATIONAL HOLIDAY
Independence Day, September 15 (1821)

TIMELINE

IN HONDURAS	IN THE WORLD
1502	
Christopher Columbus lands in Honduras.	
1520s	
Spain begins its conquest of Honduras, which is achieved in 1539.	
1700s	**1776**
The northern coast falls to British buccaneers. A British protectorate is established over the coast until 1860.	US Declaration of Independence.
	1789–1799
1821	The French Revolution.
Honduras gains independence from Spain but is absorbed into Mexico.	
1838	
Honduras becomes fully independent.	
1932–1949	**1939**
Honduras is run by the right-wing National Party of Honduras (PNH) dictatorship, led by General Tiburcio Carías Andino.	World War II begins.
	1945
1963	The United States drops atomic bombs on Hiroshima and Nagasaki. World War II ends.
After a successful coup, Colonel Oswaldo López Arellano takes power.	
1969	
Border dispute leads to a war with El Salvador.	
1981	
Roberto Suazo Córdova of the centrist Liberal Party of Honduras (PLH) is elected president, leading the first civilian government in more than a century.	
1984	**1984**
General Gustavo Álvarez is deposed amid anti-American demonstrations in Tegucigalpa.	Two bodyguards assassinate Indian prime minister Indira Gandhi.
1986	
José Azcona del Hoyo of the Liberal Party becomes president.	
1989	**1989**
General Álvarez is assassinated by left-wing guerrillas in Tegucigalpa.	The Berlin Wall falls.
1990	
Rafael Callejas sworn in as president; he introduces liberal economic reforms. The last Nicaraguan Contras leave Honduras.	

IN HONDURAS	IN THE WORLD
1997 Carlos Roberto Flores Facussé of the Liberal Party is elected president; he pledges to restructure the armed forces.	**1997** Hong Kong is returned to China.
1998 Hurricane Mitch devastates Honduras.	
2002 Ricardo Maduro is elected president.	**2001** Terrorists crash planes into New York, Washington, DC, and Pennsylvania.
	2003 The War in Iraq begins.
2005 Tropical Storm Gamma destroys homes. The Liberal Party's Manuel Zelaya is declared the winner of presidential elections.	**2005** Hundreds of people are killed when Hurricane Katrina sweeps through Gulf Coast states.
	2008 Turmoil in the US and international financial markets as major Wall Street investment bank Lehman Brothers collapses and other big US financial players face growing troubles as a result of the "credit crunch." The US faces its worst financial crisis since the Great Depression.
2009 President Manuel Zelaya is removed by the military and forced into exile. Porfirio "Pepe" Lobo Sosa of the conservative National Party wins the presidential election.	
2014 Juan Orlando Hernández takes over as president.	
2015 Tens of thousands of Hondurans march in the capital, demanding the resignation of President Hernández.	**2015** Russia intervenes in four-year-long Syrian civil war.
2016 Indigenous leader and respected environmental rights activist Berta Cáceres is killed by gunmen at her home.	**2016** UK citizens vote by referendum to leave the European Union. Donald Trump is voted president of the United States.
2017 In a disputed presidential election, incumbent Juan Orlando Hernández is declared the winner.	**2017** For the first time in ninety-nine years on August 21, a solar eclipse crosses the US from coast to coast.
2018 Juan Orlando Hernández is sworn in again as president of Honduras, while protesters are met with police violence outside of the inaugural ceremony.	**2018** Vladimir Putin is elected to his fourth term as president of Russia. President Xi Jinping of China is allowed by parliament to rule for life.

GLOSSARY

baleada (bah-lay-AH-dah)
A warm corn or flour tortilla folded over refried beans, crumbled cheese, and sour cream.

campesinos
Male peasants.

cuajada (kwah-HAH-dah)
A Honduran variety of cottage cheese.

culey (KOO-lee)
A very sweet fruit juice.

dulce de rapadura (DOOL-say de rah-pah-DUHR-ah)
Local candy made from sugarcane and wrapped in cane leaves or corn husks.

Evangélicos (eh-van-HAY-lee-kohs)
Protestant groups.

guifiti (gwee-FEE-tee)
A tea-like herbal drink.

hacendados (hah-sen-DAH-dohs)
Traditional elite who own land.

Ladino
Spanish-speaking people whose lifestyle follows Hispanic patterns.

lorena (loh-REH-nah)
A sand oven for baking breads.

machismo
Masculine behavior exhibited by men.

manta
White flowing dress material worn by the poor.

marianismo (mah-ree-ahn-EEZ-moh)
Feminine ideal emphasizing self-sacrifice and loyalty to husband and family.

mascaro (mas-KAH-roh)
Popular dance with strong African influence.

mestizo
People who are a racial mix of indigenous and European ancestry.

nacatamales (nah-kah-tah-MAH-les)
Corn cakes stuffed with vegetables and meat.

nea (NEH-ah)
A special sleeping mat.

novena
Nine nights of prayer after a family member's death and on the death anniversary.

punta (POOHN-tah)
Traditional dance of the Garifuna, performed after death; today a modern dance in discos.

tajaditas (tah-jah-DEE-tahs)
Crispy fried banana chips.

FOR FURTHER INFORMATION

BOOKS

Phillips, James J. *Honduras in Dangerous Times: Resistance and Resilience.* Lanham, MD: Lexington Books, 2015.

Preston, Douglas. *The Lost City of the Monkey God: A True Story.* New York: Grand Central Publishing, 2017.

Sjonger, Rebecca. *Cultural Traditions in Honduras.* New York: Crabtree Publishing, 2018.

Vasilyeva, Anastasiya. *Honduras.* New York, NY: Bearport Publishing, 2017.

DVDS/FILMS

Fanconi, Juan Carlos. *A Place in the Caribbean.* Cana Vista Films, 2017.

Kodath, Matthew, and Hernan Pereira. *Amor y Frijoles.* Guacamaya Films, 2009.

MUSIC

Anderson, Guillermo. *Lluvia con sol.* Costa Norte Records, 2012.

Banda Blanc. *Saben Quien Llego.* M-Gen Stream, 2015.

Cortés, Eva. *Crossing Borders.* Origin Records, 2017.

BIBLIOGRAPHY

BOOKS

Alvarez, Miguel O. *Integral Mission: A Paradigm for Latin American Pentecostals*. Oxford, UK: Regnum Books, 2016.

Ashlie, Malana. *Gringos in Paradise: Our Honduras Odyssey*. Charleston, SC: BookSurge Publishing, 2007.

Chandler, Gary, and Liza Prado. *Honduras & the Bay Islands*. Oakland, CA: Lonely Planet, 2007.

Gollin, James D. *Adventures in Nature: Honduras*. Adventures in Nature series. Emeryville, CA: Avalon Travel Publishing, 2001.

Humphrey, Chris. *Honduras*. Moon Handbooks. Emeryville, CA: Avalon Travel Publishing, 2006.

WEBSITES

BBC News, http://www.bbc.com/news/world-latin-america-18954311.

Britannica, https://www.britannica.com/place/Honduras.

CIA World Factbook, https://www.cia.gov/library/publications/resources/the-world-factbook/geos/ho.html.

Country Studies, http://countrystudies.us/honduras/38.htm.

Encyclopedia of the Nations—Honduras, http://www.nationsencyclopedia.com/economies/Americas/Honduras.html.

INDEX

INDEX